TV News

Building a Career
in Broadcast Journalism

Ray White

Focal Press
Boston London

Focal Press is an imprint of Butterworth Publishers.

Library of Congress Cataloging-in-Publication Data

White, Ray.
   TV news : building a career in broadcast
   journalism / Ray White.
       p.   cm.
   Includes bibliographical references.
   ISBN 0-240-80036-2
   1. Television broadcasting of news—Vocational guid-
       ance.   2. Journalism—Vocational
       guidance.   I. Title.
   PN4784.T4W48   1990
   070.1'95—dc20   89-37486

British Library Cataloguing in Publication Data

White, Ray
   TV News : building a career in broadcast journalism.
   1. Television programmes: News programmes.
       Journalism
   I. Title
   070.1'9

ISBN 0-240-80036-2

Butterworth Publishers
80 Montvale Avenue
Stoneham, MA 02180

10 9 8 7 6 5 4 3 2 1

Printed in the United States of America

This book is dedicated to my wife
Bonnie,
whose help made *TV News* possible.
It's also dedicated to
my daughter Lauri
and son David,
of whom we're extremely proud.

Contents

Preface

Since the mid-seventies, the number of journalism students on the nation's college campuses has increased substantially. It seems that as the dominance of TV news grew, so did the number of students wanting to make this exciting field their career. Until the early 1970s, however, quite a few schools didn't offer journalism majors (in the early years, many people in TV news on the local level had come from the ranks of radio announcers). But as stations expanded their news departments and the demand for trained newspeople increased, colleges and universities responded and supplied larger numbers of journalists for the business. Today, it is unusual for someone to be hired in TV news without a college degree. Often the degree is in journalism, but if not, the person has a strong journalism minor or a great deal of practical experience.

As you'll see in Chapter 1, "TV News Today," the industry has undergone a number of changes. Like most other businesses, it's had to tighten its belt in recent years because of increased competition and inflationary costs. Because of network layoffs in the mid-eighties, hundreds of TV news jobs have probably been lost for good. In addition to the networks, a number of larger stations had to either scale down the size of their news departments or postpone plans to expand. This change, viewed by many as negative, may have been a big factor in causing some TV newspeople in the larger markets to sign longer-term contracts in order to gain more job security. Because of these factors, career advancement in the field is somewhat slower today than it was a decade ago.

Because so many young people have decided on TV journalism as a career, today's journalism students will be going after fewer jobs than in the past and facing more competition for those positions. If you want to break into the field, you will obviously have to do something to make yourself stand out from the others—and that means getting as much training, exposure, and experience in TV news as possible before you graduate from college.

I've spent 20 years in the business. As a news director, I've come into contact with hundreds of journalism students and new graduates, especially in the past decade. Many of them have asked the same questions about the inner workings of TV news.

A number of these questions can be answered through experience as an intern. Unfortunately, many students can't work in a TV newsroom in any capacity before they graduate. Even during an internship, a student may not be able to learn everything necessary about the practical side of the business. Access to some basic information even before interning will help many students prepare for, and take full advantage of, an internship. Perhaps just as important, informed students will be able to refine their career objectives at an early stage of their education.

TV News is a supplemental text designed to help students understand what a career in TV journalism entails and what they can expect after graduation. It brings the real world of TV news to the student who may not have had the chance to spend some time in a newsroom. This book does not teach journalism; that's the job of your college or university. Rather, it is intended to give you a practical understanding of the industry—an understanding usually gained only through on-the-job experience.

TV News is written especially for college journalism students and others who are considering entering the field. But it can also serve as a valuable handbook for journalism graduates: we discuss such topics as how to go about job hunting and what news directors really look for in cover letters, résumés, and videotapes. Even if you've interned in a TV newsroom, you'll find that this book contains a lot of practical information you need to know.

This book is divided into five parts. Part I takes a brief look at the history of the business, from its beginnings in the 1950s to today's computerized newsrooms and satellite live shots.

In Part II you'll learn about the jobs in a TV newsroom—what various people do and where their career might lead them next in TV news. This section covers a number of common terms that are used almost every day. It also describes how newsrooms of various sizes are organized: who does what, and how duties and responsibilities increase in smaller news departments. Chapter 6 takes you through a typical day, from 5 A.M. until past the 11 o'clock newscast. You'll see what happens in the newsroom as the day's events unfold and plans are changed in order to get the news covered.

Part III deals with three terms you may have heard: *markets*, *ratings*, and *consultants*. These complex and important topics are discussed in detail in separate chapters. They all can affect your career and your salary.

Part IV concerns assessing your basic abilities and attributes and preparing yourself for the business through college training, internships, and other activities. It also contains pointers on gaining access to a TV newsroom and suggests what you can do on campus and off to prepare yourself for a news career. The all-important chapter "Your First News Job" provides a lot of useful and practical information that could make landing your first job a little easier.

Part V discusses your future in the business as it relates to specific jobs in the newsroom and identifies the jobs that are most (and least) stable. Finally, Chapter 15, "Career Changes and Alternatives," suggests some other fields you might consider if you leave TV news.

Deciding on what career to pursue is one of the most important things you'll ever do. I hope *TV News* helps you make that decision, and wish you the best of luck. Who knows—one day you may be one of the top-paid correspondents, or even a network anchor. The jobs will have to be filled by someone—maybe you!

TV News

I AN OVERVIEW

1 TV News Today

A TV news career can be an extremely exciting and rewarding experience. You'll meet people in high places and find that your membership in the press allows you special considerations in many situations. Almost everyone in the business will say that their status as a reporter has enabled them to go places and do things they had never thought possible. There's no doubt about it—being a reporter is sometimes a heady experience.

Although you may arrive at work at the same time as many of your friends in other jobs, your day will most likely have more variety than theirs. From the smallest towns to the largest cities, TV journalism offers a constantly changing diet of news to cover. Not every day is dramatically different from the last, but a TV journalist knows how varied just one week's worth of news coverage can be. It's a variety that's hard to find in other fields.

As might be expected, TV journalism is often a difficult field. What makes the job exciting—the variety, the unique experiences, the pleasure of communicating to thousands (or millions) of people—also makes it extremely demanding (Figure 1.1). Changes in the industry during the last decade have made the profession even more demanding. These changes have also made TV news one of the most competitive fields for newcomers.

The "Golden Years"

Many TV newspeople look back with special fondness on the 1970s and early 1980s. Some might call them the "golden years." They were good times for both network news departments and local newsrooms. During this era, network news divisions expanded their staffs and opened new bureaus to provide more extensive news coverage. Although network anchors were paid well in the early seventies, their salaries skyrocketed in the last half of the decade. You may recall Barbara Walters' lucrative contract when she switched from NBC to ABC

FIGURE 1.1. A typical television newsroom today. Each reporter's work station is crowded with telephone number lists, books, pamphlets, and other items collected while covering stories. Television sets on the back wall monitor what's being aired on the other stations in the city. The lights rarely go out in this newsroom because it's a 24-hour operation, staffed all the time.

during this period. Other high salaries for network anchors followed, but hers was probably the first to receive so much publicity. Many local anchors, especially in the larger cities, were being paid well too.

The television advertising business was thriving, and sponsors were spending a lot of money to advertise on successful network shows. This made it easier for the networks to spend money on expansion, especially in their news departments. Meanwhile, many local stations were increasing the sophistication of their newscasts and adding specialists, such as medical, consumer, or investigative reporters, to their staffs. A number of stations expanded their newscasts from a half hour to a full hour, or added a second half hour that either preceded or followed their network newscast. Because of this expansion in the TV news business, people were able to move up the career ladder swiftly.

It was an exciting time from a technological standpoint, too. Stations were switching from film to videotape (more about tape, and equipment in general, in Chapter 2). Some stations were equipped with live units—specially outfitted vans or trucks equipped with microwave TV transmitters. Live units opened up a whole new electronic universe and added greatly to stations' ability to cover the news.

In the early 1980s, however, network executives realized that a new type of competition was growing rapidly. Cable TV, which was not much of a presence in the late seventies, was now taking a larger and larger share of the TV audience. The big three networks combined had always been able to get into most of America's homes at some time during the day or evening. But the new figures were ominous; cable was taking a bigger bite out of the television audience each year. No one cable channel had a notably large audience, but all of them together represented a sizeable share of viewers. It became obvious that the competition was going to get tougher as more people opted for cable TV. Cable programming is competition for all network and affiliate programming, including both network and local newscasts.

The sales explosion of home videocassette recorders (VCRs), along with movie rentals, has also lured away a percentage of network viewers. Many people who have cable and a VCR tape movies and other shows during the day while they're at work and watch them that night, rather than network TV. Of course, this doesn't happen all the time, but an average of even one night a week per family concerns network executives.

The networks found themselves with a perplexing situation—increasing costs due to inflation *and* more competition. Also, by the mid-eighties, new owners had taken over CBS, NBC, and ABC. As cost-conscious executives who saw too much "fat" in their respective networks, they made sizeable reductions in staff and imposed other budgetary restraints. Some employees were laid off; others took early retirements. Most of the media publications speculated that each network would lose at least a thousand people. Cuts were made in many departments, including the news divisions. This must have been a bitter pill for network news executives to swallow, since they had known only expansion in their departments, never cutbacks. Sadly, those cut positions are probably gone forever.

This was distressing news for local TV journalists because many of the laid-off network people were looking for jobs almost anywhere. Naturally, they filtered into openings in medium and larger markets; some even took smaller-market positions. As a result, anyone trying to move up in the business in the mid-eighties encountered more competition than ever before. There were fewer openings and plenty of leftover network people to apply for them. As you might imagine, this hindered upward career mobility, even in the small markets. Fortunately, most of those who were laid off at the networks had either found other jobs in the business or had gotten out of TV completely by 1989.

How Does the State of the Industry Affect You?

What does all this mean to you, as someone exploring the possibility of becoming a TV journalist? For one thing, local stations are not expanding their news departments as many news directors would like, and in many cases expansion plans have been cancelled. In an effort to cut their budgets, some news departments have even eliminated a position or two. Also, the usual raises given today aren't nearly as big as those awarded in past years. You need to remember that in most cases local stations face the same problems (although on a smaller scale) as the networks. That's because the networks are made up of local affiliates. If a network show is doing badly, it's getting low ratings in many cities. This means the station is making fewer advertising dollars and thus has less money to pass around when raises are due or equipment has to be purchased.

If you enter the business now, you need to have a love of reporting, because you may not be lucky enough to move to the anchor desk. You may ask, "What's not to love?" Well, that's an understandable question, because there is certainly something special about the business. But despite the way TV reporters are portrayed on television and in the movies, it's not as glamorous a life as you might think (except, perhaps, in the top markets or networks).

Because of all the recent changes in TV news, it's more important than ever to be well prepared when you leave school and embark on your career. Part of this preparation is becoming knowledgeable about the realities of TV news and what you can expect.

Despite some rough times, TV news is still alive and well. Even some of the network news executives had said budgets were too fat and costs had gotten out of hand. Perhaps it was time to trim things down. When you stop and think about it, today's network newscasts and local news programs are generally done as well as they were in the early eighties.

2 Technology—Then and Now

What we see today on TV is a far cry from the first TV newscasts of the early 1950s. Back then, photographers rushed from one location to another to capture events on black-and-white film. This was the first type of on-the-scene coverage of events, used by both networks and local stations around the country. Today we have videotape, live reports, computers, and satellite news-gathering equipment—advances that two decades ago would have seemed like they were out of *Buck Rogers*. TV news is inherently dependent on technology. Thus, every good television journalist has a solid knowledge of the equipment used in the industry. Let's take a brief look at how far we've come in the technology of TV news.

Optical Sound Cameras

If you compare old newsfilm from the 1950s with modern broadcasts, you'd really notice a difference. The picture of the old newsfilm would be acceptable, but the sound quality would be poor at best by today's standards. The cameras used in the fifties, equipped with optical sound recorders, seem archaic today. Many stations used this gear through the late sixties, although the more forward-thinking had already converted to the next generation of equipment.

Magnetic Sound

New technology solved the audio problem and brought us magnetic ("mag") sound. This was a big step forward for news departments. The high quality of magnetic sound, together with color film, increased the feeling of "being there" while watching a news story. The camera, equipped with a recording amplifier, microphone, and battery, was a compact unit weighing around 16 pounds. The only other item a photographer needed was a battery belt to power a portable light (mounted on the camera) in case anything had to be filmed at night. With this equipment, a photographer could go anywhere—day or night—and bring back the story in color, with improved sound. But more was to come.

Videotape

The magnetic-sound film cameras enjoyed their heyday in the sixties and early seventies, but by the mid-seventies portable videotape gear was being marketed, and a number of stations purchased it. Even though TV stations had been using videotape for years to record commercials and network shows, lightweight equipment that was compact enough to take out in the field to cover news events had not been produced until that time. By 1980 most news departments had gotten away from film altogether and were using portable videotape gear, commonly called *electronic news-gathering (ENG) gear* (Figure 2.1).

This vastly improved equipment revolutionized TV news video. The portable videotape camera produced a sharper image than many film cameras, and sound quality was also better with the latest electronics (ENG gear uses magnetic sound too). But one of the biggest advantages was that there was no film to develop. Film must be processed first and then edited, which can take hours; with videotape, you can edit right after you shoot. That a videotaped story can be edited immediately is obviously of crucial importance in TV news.

Although the basic qualities of videotape make it the ideal medium for journalism, film is still used for many commercials and has other uses as well. Filmed images have a "soft" look that many commercial producers prefer; they are not quite as sharp and clear as videotaped images.

The videotape loaded into the portable ENG recorder comes in 20-minute videocassettes (special 30-minute versions are also available). The tape is three-quarters of an inch wide, in contrast to the one- and two-inch tapes used in the studio. But the big difference is that unlike the tape used in the studio, which is generally stored on open reels, this tape is enclosed in a plastic videocassette body and does not need to be threaded into the recorder. The threading of the videotape on a cassette is an automatic process when the videocassette is inserted into the tape-recorder mechanism. Despite the obvious advantages of this early videotape gear, it still has one significant drawback: its weight. Remember, the magnetic-sound film camera was a single unit weighing about 16 pounds with camera, recorder, and battery rolled into one. Videotape gear uses a camera that weighs 15 to 20 pounds, but the backbreaker is the recorder, which weighs more than 25 pounds. You can imagine how

FIGURE 2.1. An ENG videotape camera (center), a videotape recorder in its carrying case (right), and a battery belt with a portable light (left). Behind the camera is a heavy-duty tripod that's seen a lot of use. The one portable light is fine for quick interviews, but for special situations the photographer would instead use up to three portable lights (not shown) that plug into standard AC electrical outlets. These provide better lighting of the subject and eliminate concern about battery failure.

tough it is for photographers to use this equipment. This type of ENG equipment is still in wide use today, although a number of stations have converted to the next generation of videotape gear—Betacam.

Betacam

Fortunately, by the early 1980s, the Betacam was introduced by Sony. The Betacam is probably the most widely used self-contained videotape camera-recorder in TV news today, although it's not the only brand available. In a way, it is similar to the film cameras of the 1960s. It's a videotape camera, recorder, and battery all in one unit that weighs under 20 pounds. Compared with the excessively heavy videotape gear of the seventies and early eighties, the Betacam obviously makes the photographer's job a lot easier. With this equipment, for the first time since film days, a photographer can just be a photographer again, instead of a combination baggage handler–photographer. The videotape used in the Betacam is half an inch wide and comes loaded in plastic video-cassettes, much like the tapes in home video systems.

The Betacam technology was a real breakthrough. Many news departments have either made the change to this equipment or plan to. The benefits are really appreciated by the newsperson who is both a reporter and photographer combined (more about "one-man bands" in Chapter 4).

Live Shots

Another breakthrough in news coverage was the live report, commonly called a *live shot*. We've seen live shots on the networks for years, but they weren't common on most local stations until the mid-to-late seventies, or even the early eighties in some cases. Stations in many small markets today still don't have *live units*.

Basically, a live unit (or *live van*) is a specially outfitted van or truck equipped with a microwave TV transmitter (Figure 2.2). This is a type of transmitter that sends both picture and sound in a straight line-of-sight signal to a TV station or its television transmission tower. Microwave transmitters must be used for live shots. Because TV stations send out their main signals on one frequency, they need additional, special frequencies so the signals from their live reports won't intefere with the main signal. A camera and microphone are plugged into the microwave transmitter, and the signal is sent back to either the studio or the station's tower. Most live shots are sent to the tower and then rerouted to the studio, where they go through the same equipment as everything else in the newscast.

On top of the live van is a tall antenna that looks something like a giant telescope, usually mounted on a mast. The operator can run the mast nearly 50 feet up (depending on the size of the mast) and position the antenna so it can transmit in any direction. This allows the signal to travel above anything on the ground that might interrupt its transmission. Signals from live vans have to go in a straight line to their target receiver on the TV tower, unlike regular broadcast signals, which can be received almost anywhere in an area. In rough terrain full of hills and valleys, a live shot may be impossible.

Live vans can cost more than $100,000, but some TV engineering departments have put them together for much less than that. Even though the simpler units may not have all the refinements, they still do the job. All live vans have

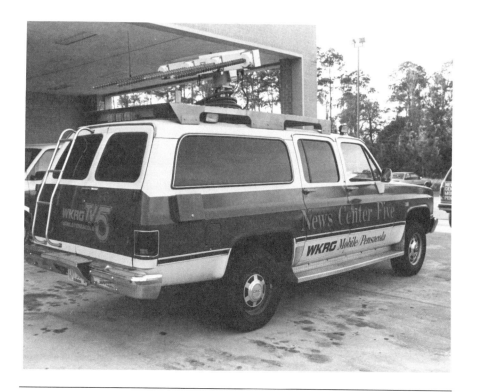

FIGURE 2.2. This live unit is similar to many used by television stations throughout the country. The truck has a generator on board that powers everything, including the exterior lights. On top is a special telescoping mast with a microwave transmission antenna. The mast is raised until it is higher than surrounding trees and buildings so that the best possible picture may be transmitted to the station. Inside the truck is a microwave transmitter and other gear that the TV station finds useful in its live units.

a generator on board to run the equipment, because in many cases finding standard AC electrical outlets is impossible. Even if power is nearby, it may be very difficult to locate someone who will give you permission to use it. As you might imagine, many live shots originate in areas where there is no AC outlet at all.

Although it is a significant advance, live reporting is really just another tool that's required from time to time to do a better job of telling the story. Live reports are sometimes the only way a story can be covered. This is especially true when the story is occurring while a newscast is underway. If that's the case, a report transmitted live from the scene is certainly the most effective, if not the only, way to tell viewers what's happening.

Let's say a big fire breaks out in the downtown area around 11 A.M., requiring the evacuation of hundreds of workers. If a station has a live van, a live report should be done as soon as possible (as a cut-in to regular network programming) because of the fire's seriousness. Other live reports might be made throughout the day to update viewers. Then that night at 6 o'clock, the reporter covering the story might do another live shot from the scene with the latest information.

Live shots frequently occur while the story itself is in progress. For example, at a school board meeting that began at 5 or 6 P.M., a reporter could do a live report while the meeting is underway, perhaps with an interview of someone involved in it.

Many stations make every effort to use live reports as often as possible, whereas others use them less frequently. But if the competition has live capability and uses it effectively, the station without it is at a disadvantage.

Satellites and Satellite News Trucks

Satellites are revolutionizing many aspects of television and certainly are providing many new opportunities for TV journalists. At present, there are about two dozen commercial TV satellites orbiting the earth. Each satellite usually carries 24 *transponders*, devices that actually receive and transmit signals from the earth. Generally, a transponder can relay one standard television signal or a number of voice (telephone) channels at any given moment. With use of a satellite, television signals can be transmitted great distances, surpassing the line-of-sight limitations of microwave transmissions. Satellites also offer greater capacity than other means of transmitting signals.

Of course, to take advantage of this marvelous technology, a station must have the necessary satellite transmission and reception equipment. Most stations do today; the networks had converted to satellite transmission by the mid-eighties, and the affiliates followed suit shortly. A great many of the transponders on satellites are owned by private companies, which in turn lease the use of the transponders to other companies. This allows news sources other than the networks to transmit stories to stations.

Many stations have bureaus in Washington, D.C., to cover items of local interest that occur in Washington (local congressional representatives voting on a controversial bill, for example). In the past, these stories were shot on film or videotape, which was then sent back to the station by plane. This caused obvious problems as far as timeliness was concerned; sometimes the story reached the station the next day, almost too late to air. But now, if a story happens in (for example) Washington at 7 P.M., the news crew there can get the story, edit it, and feed it by satellite to the station at 10:30 that night if necessary (more about feeds in Chapter 3). In effect, satellites have opened up "instant networks" that weren't there before.

The latest addition to the arsenal of news-gathering equipment is the *satellite truck*, also referred to as a *satellite news vehicle*, or SNV (Figures 2.3 and 2.4). A satellite truck may resemble a live unit to the untrained eye and, in many ways, it is similar; the difference is how it gets the signal back to the studio.

You'll recall that it is impossible to send a live report from a live van if the terrain is too rough, because the signal has to be sent in a straight line to the station or TV tower. If the live van operator can't position the transmitting antenna to "see" the tower in a line-of-sight manner, a live shot will not be possible.

FIGURE 2.3. This satellite truck has its large transmission dish aimed at one of the satellites circling the earth. Trucks such as this have an amazing amount of electronic gear on board. Normally, the truck will carry two of everything, so if one piece of equipment breaks down, the operator can simply switch to the backup unit.

FIGURE 2.4. The interior of the satellite truck shown in Figure 2.3. Behind the panel is the transmitter that sends the TV signal through the satellite dish. Like live units (as shown in Figure 2.2), these trucks can send videotape or a live TV signal originating from a camera plugged into the truck.

However, with a satellite truck, a live shot is almost always feasible. The truck can be located almost anywhere and still get its signal back to the station. How? The truck sends its signal to one of the many satellites circling the earth, avoiding virtually all obstacles. From there, the signal is transmitted back to earth, where the TV station receives it by means of a satellite dish. It may then be included in the newscast like any other live shot. Regardless of the type of truck being used, the reporter and photographer cover the story in roughly the same manner. Like live vans, satellite trucks have a generator on board if power is needed.

Satellite trucks were introduced in the early eighties, but by the late eighties most stations still did not have one. One big reason is the high cost —usually over $275,000.

Computerized Newsrooms

Computers have had quite an impact on the way reporters receive and prepare news for broadcasting. A computer system not only efficiently ties together the reporters and resources of a newsroom but may also link the newsroom to other newsrooms and sources of information all over the country and the world (Figure 2.5).

Although many newsrooms still don't have computers, their station's accounting department has probably had one for quite some time. But that computer may be used only for the station's accounting and billing purposes and is probably nothing like one that might be hooked up in the newsroom. So when you hear that a station has a computer, find out whether it has a newsroom computer system or not.

FIGURE 2.5. Computers are seen more and more in television newsrooms these days. They make a number of tasks easier and quicker, and they allow people to concentrate on writing and producing better newscasts.

An important aspect of the computerized newsroom is the way it manages copy from independent news services (*wire services*) such as the Associated Press (AP) and United Press International (UPI). These companies provide extensive local, national, and international news to newspapers and radio and TV stations that subscribe to their services. (In the past, this copy was transmitted to special printers, called wire machines, in the subscribing newspaper office or station.)

At most computerized TV stations, stories from the wire services are transmitted directly into the computer system, where they are accepted and stored chronologically. At a computer console you can scan all the wires. If you're looking for a particular story, you can view only wires in the applicable category, such as state, national, world, sports, weather, or business news. You can get even more specific by having the computer search for the name of a person, or a location, or some other key word in the story. This is a great timesaver.

Many computer systems offer an additional feature. Once you've found the story you want, you can view a split screen, with the story you've selected on one side of the screen and a blank "page" on the other. You can then rewrite the story on one half of the screen while looking at the wire copy on the other. You can also write local stories (not based on wire-service copy) on the computer, much as you would on a word processor.

Perhaps one of the biggest advantages of computers is that they permit easier rewriting, which makes for a more understandable story. Computers also eliminate a lot of time-consuming paper handling. In more advanced applications, computers can operate the TelePrompTer from which anchors read during the newscast (the TelePrompTer is discussed in Chapter 3). For producers, computers make planning and timing a newscast go much faster.

Newsroom computers do a lot; we have covered only a sampling. If technology advances as fast in TV news as it has in most other areas of broadcasting, there's no telling what the 1990s will bring.

II HOW NEWSROOMS OPERATE

3 TV Newsroom Terms

Like people in many other professions, those who work in a newsroom have their own lingo that may sound strange to outsiders. This chapter covers many common newsroom terms that are used constantly and are essential for you to know.

Figure 3.1 shows a sample *newscast rundown*, which lists all the stories to be aired on a particular show. The rundown and the stories themselves are fairly representative of what you'll find in the industry, although there may be slight variations from station to station. Five basic types of news scripts are found in a newscast. As I describe them, I will also discuss some of the technology used to create them. I will then detail broad story elements and formats, as well as a few basic concepts concerning the organization and operation of TV stations and news departments.

The Five Basic News Scripts

Reader

The most basic news story is a *reader*, or *liner* (Figure 3.2). This is a story read on camera by one of the anchors, with no videotape appearing on the screen while the anchor is talking. A picture or *graphic* (drawing) may or may not be shown over the anchor's shoulder by an electronic process generally called *keying* or *inserting*. Most news departments prefer that a reader not be too long (25 seconds or less) unless it's an extremely important story that broke late, making it impossible to get video on the air.

Supers are important elements to every story with video in it. Supers are names or other bits of information superimposed on the TV screen. They're generally classified as either *locators* or *identifiers*. Locator supers indicate the

SG#	SLUG	CUES		TAPE	STORY TIME	CUME	LEFT
	6PM NEWS					6:00:00	30:00
A 1	NEWS OPEN				:20	6:00:20	29:40
A 2	WOODS FIRE	RAY/STR/TAPE	ST-TAG	G-56	1:40	6:02:00	28:00
A 3	BANK ROBBERY	KJ/STR/TAPE	ST-TAG	N-56	:20	6:02:20	27:40
A 4	PRISON ESCAPEES	KJ/SS		RDR.	:20	6:02:40	27:20
A 5	SHERIFF'S TRIAL	KJ/STR/TAPE	ST-TAG	C43	1:45	6:04:25	25:35
A 6	POLICE CHIEF SHOT	RAY/STR		RDR.	:20	6:04:45	25:15
A 7	TOXIC AIR	RAY/SS/TAPE	ST-TAG	B-26	1:40	6:06:25	23:35
A 8	TEASE ONE	2-SHOT/TAPE KJ/RAY			:20	6:06:45	23:15
A 9	BREAK ONE	WILLIAMS AUTO SHOP			2:00	6:08:45	21:15
B10	CONVENTION CENTER	KJ/SS/TAPE	ST-TAG	H-22	1:35	6:10:20	19:40
B11	LIQUOR CRACKDOWN	RAY/SS/TAPE	ST-TAG	N-34	:45	6:11:05	18:55
B12	LIBRARY RULES	RAY/STR/TAPE	ST-TAG	D-23	:20	6:11:25	18:35
B13	TEACHER AWARDS	RAY/SS/TAPE	ST-TAG	F16	:45	6:12:10	17:50
B14	MISS U.S.A.	KJ/SS/TAPE	ST-TAG	G-21	1:40	6:13:50	16:10
B15	TEASE TWO	2-SHOT/TAPE RAY/KJ			:20	6:14:10	15:50
B16	BREAK TWO	EDWARDS TOYS			2:00	6:16:10	13:50
C17	WEATHER	KJ/BILL			3:45	6:19:55	10:05
C18	TEASE THREE	2-SHOT/TAPE RAY/KJ			:20	6:20:15	9:45
C19	BREAK THREE	AMMERBY'S			2:00	6:22:15	7:45
D20	SPORTS	RAY/BOB			3:30	6:25:45	4:15
D21	TEASE FOUR	2-SHOT/TAPE KJ/RAY			:20	6:26:05	3:55
D22	BREAK FOUR	TWO-FOR-ONE			2:00	6:28:05	1:55
E23	COMPUTER TOYS	KJ/STR/TAPE			1:40	6:29:45	:15
E24	(SAY GOODBYE)	RAY/KJ			:15	6:30:00	0:00

END OF NEWSCAST - JOIN NETWORK

FIGURE 3.1. In this newscast rundown, the newscast is broken down into sections A, B, C, D, and E. Sections A and B are devoted to news, section C to weather, section D to sports, and section E, the closing section, to lighter news. Each element of the newscast, including commercials, has a segment number (SG#), shown in the far left column. The SLUG column lists the title of each story. The CUES column indicates which anchor will read the story and whether the anchor will be shown "straight on camera" (STR) or with a picture or *graphic* (drawing) over the shoulder (SS). SS stands for *still store*, an electronic process that is one of several ways to put pictures or graphics on the screen along with the anchor. ST-TAG means the anchor will wind up on camera reading a sentence or two to conclude the story after the videotape for that story ends. Each listing in the CUES column that corresponds to a break listed in the SLUG column (break one, two, three, or four) identifies the last commercial to be shown in that break before returning to the studio (the average break contains four 30-second commercials). Where applicable, the TAPE column indicates the number of the videotape that contains a story. RDR means the story is a *reader*—that is, there is no videotape; the anchor reads the entire story on camera. The STORY TIME column lists the estimated total time of the story in minutes and seconds, including the anchor lead-in and tag. The CUME column shows the running time of the newscast after each story has concluded, and the LEFT column indicates the total time left in the newscast after each story (in both cases, assuming that the story times are correct). Especially toward the end of a newscast, this information can help the producer decide whether it is necessary to shorten something in order to end the newscast on time.

```
                    READER SCRIPT
                      ( RDR )


SG#   SLUG                    CUES             STORY TIME
A6    POLICE CHIEF SHOT       RAY/STR             :20
================================================================
RAY/STRAIGHT                      THE TIPTON POLICE CHIEF IS IN STABLE
                                  CONDITION TONIGHT AFTER BEING SHOT IN
                                  THE STOMACH TODAY.  THE SHOOTING
                                  OCCURRED WHEN A MAN FLED THE EDWARDS
                                  COUNTY COURTHOUSE IN TIPTON AFTER
                                  REPORTEDLY FIRING SHOTS IN THE
                                  SHERIFF'S OFFICE.  HE WAS CONFRONTED
                                  OUTSIDE THE COURTHOUSE BY TIPTON
                                  POLICE CHIEF SAM PULLAM.  AT THAT
                                  POINT, POLICE SAY PULLAM WAS SHOT.
                                  AUTHORITIES ARE LOOKING FOR A KNOWN
                                  SUSPECT IN THE CASE.
```

FIGURE 3.2. A reader script from the sample newscast outlined in the rundown in Figure 3.1. The SG# column shows that the story runs in segment A and is the sixth element in the newscast. The CUES listing indicates that the anchor will be on camera straight (STR). In other words, no graphic or picture will be inserted over the anchor's shoulder—the story is strictly a straight reader.

location where the story or a part of it was shot. Identifier supers show the name of the person seen talking on the screen.

A *character generator* (*CG* for short) is an electronic device that puts letters and numbers on a TV picture, just as a typewriter puts them on a piece of paper. Many electronic devices in today's TV stations can do much more— even "paint" a picture. But the character generator is responsible for most of the words and numbers superimposed on TV pictures.

Voice-Over

The *voice-over*, or *VO*, is similar to the reader but includes video. Figure 3.3 shows an example of a VO script. Shortly after the anchor begins a story on camera, videotape of the story appears on the screen while the anchor continues to read. When the tape first appears on the screen, you will see the name of the place where it was shot—the locator super. If the tape is edited properly, the videotaped images will match what the anchor is talking about. Shortly before the end of the story, the anchor is back on camera with a final sentence to wrap it up. This is commonly called *tagging* the story. The script may or may not call for a *key*, or *insert*, over the anchor's shoulder at the beginning or end. Sometimes the video used on a VO consists only of graphics or charts,

```
SG#    SLUG               CUES                      STORY TIME
A3     BANK ROBBERY       KJ/STR/TAPE ST-TAG           :20
================================================================================
KJ/STRAIGHT                              TODAY, ANOTHER BANK ROBBERY IN
                                         LAWRENCEVILLE, AND THAT BRINGS THE
TAKE TAPE                                TOTAL NUMBER OF BANK HEISTS THIS YEAR
super: Today, Lawrenceville              TO EIGHT.  A HAMILTON BANK BRANCH AT
              :01-:06                     THE CORNER OF COTTAGE HILL AND
                                         WILLIAMS STREET WAS ROBBED THIS
                                         MORNING OF AN UNDETERMINED AMOUNT OF
                                         MONEY.  POLICE ARE LOOKING FOR A WHITE
                                         MALE, AROUND 30, WITH BLONDISH HAIR
                                         AND A STOCKY BUILD.  THE BANDIT WAS
TAPE OUT-KJ/STRAIGHT                     LAST SEEN RUNNING THROUGH A PARKING
                                         LOT NEXT TO THE BANK.
```

FIGURE 3.3. A voice-over script, more commonly referred to as a VO, from the sample newscast outlined in Figure 3.1. The SG# column shows that the story runs in segment A and is the third element in the newscast. The CUES listing shows that the story will start with the anchor on camera straight (STR), followed by a videotape (TAPE), and will end with a straight tag (ST-TAG). On the right side of the script is the copy the anchor will read. On the left side are directions for the newscast director. The super for the story is indicated—in this case, a locator ("Today, Lawrenceville")—along with the time the director should put it on the screen (from one to six seconds into the tape). Prior to the newscast, the director will ensure that all the locator and identifier supers are typed into the character generator. The story will go to video after the anchor has been on camera for about five seconds. Around the anchor's words "a stocky build," the director will get ready to drop the videotape and go to the anchor again for the straight tag—a concluding statement with no graphic or picture.

as opposed to *moving video* showing people, places, or things. In other cases, the video consists of information put on the screen by the character generator.

A *tag* is a concluding statement an anchor makes to end a story (*tag out*). If an anchor goes directly from one story to another, viewers may not always be aware that one story has ended and the next one has begun. But with a tag (which should be an informative statement, not merely a contrived wrap-up sentence), viewers will realize the story has ended. Tags are especially helpful in stories that include *sound bites* or *VO bites*.

Sound Bite

A *sound bite*, or *cold bite*, is a type of story that includes no videotape of the story itself (as does a VO) but does include a brief videotaped interview with someone knowledgeable about the story. A sound-bite script is shown in Figure 3.4. The anchor begins on-camera and reads to a certain point in the script; then someone appears on videotape, making a comment relative to the story (with the proper name-identifier super on the screen). At the end of the sound bite the anchor reappears to tag the story before moving on to another. A typical sound bite might consist of a congressional representative's comments about a bill under debate in Congress and how it may affect the district or the nation. In stories on such subjects, sound bites are often the only video available.

<pre>
                        SOUND BITE SCRIPT
                           (BITE)

SG#   SLUG   CUES   STORY TIME
B11   LIQUOR CRACKDOWN   RAY/SS/TAPE ST-TAG   :45
==
RAY/SS   LOCAL ALCOHOL BEVERAGE CONTROL
                                                OFFICIALS SAY THEY'RE CONCERNED OVER
                                                THE NUMBER OF PEOPLE BUYING ALCOHOL
                                                ACROSS STATE LINES TO AVOID PAYING
                                                TAXES ON IT. BUT THEY SAY THEIR MAIN
                                                TARGETS ARE THOSE WHO BRING IN LARGE
                                                QUANTITIES. AGENT FRED WILLIAMSON
                                                SAYS MUCH OF THE OUT-OF-STATE LIQUOR
                                                IS BROUGHT IN BY BOOTLEGGERS WHO
                                                RESELL THE BEVERAGES IN NON-
                                                LICENSED BUSINESSES OR IN DRY
                                                COUNTIES.
TAKE TAPE/SOUND UP TILL :16
super: Outcue.."..stamp on them."
 Fred Williamson, A.B.C. Agent :01-:06
TAG-RAY/STRAIGHT   TONIGHT ON NEWSCENTER AT 10 WE'LL
                                                EXAMINE THE LIQUOR TAX AND HOW
                                                EXTENSIVE THE PROBLEM IS OF PEOPLE
                                                BUYING OUT OF STATE.
</pre>

FIGURE 3.4. A sound-bite script from the sample newscast outlined in Figure 3.1. The SG# column shows that the story is in segment B and is the eleventh element in the newscast. The CUES listing shows that it begins with a picture over the anchor's shoulder (SS), goes to videotape (TAPE), and winds up with a straight tag (ST-TAG). On the right side of the script is the copy the anchor will read (except for the outcue —the last few words of the sound bite). On the left side are directions for the newscast director. In this case, a picture will appear over the anchor's shoulder during the lead-in to the sound bite. The script tells the director when to take, or go to, the videotape with sound up (TAKE TAPE/SOUND UP TILL)—immediately after the anchor says "in dry counties." The length of the sound bite is 16 seconds. At the outcue, "stamp on them," the anchor will reappear on camera for a straight tag. The super used in this story is a name identifier (Fred Williamson, A.B.C. Agent) rather than a locator. This is simply because there is no location to identify prior to the sound bite.

Voice-Over/Sound Bite

The *voice-over/sound bite*, or *VO-bite*, is a combination of the VO and the sound bite (Figure 3.5 shows a sample script). The story begins like a VO, but at some point the anchor stops reading, and a sound bite with someone involved in the story or knowledgeable about it appears on camera. After the sound bite there may be more footage of the same story, with the anchor continuing to narrate, or the anchor may be back on camera immediately after the bite to end the story. As with the VO and the sound bite, a VO-bite should always conclude with the anchor tagging out. Both a locator super and a name-identifier super will be found in the VO-bite.

```
                       VOICE-OVER/SOUND BITE SCRIPT
                              ( VO-bite )


SG#    SLUG                  CUES                     STORY TIME
B13    TEACHER AWARDS        RAY/SS/TAPE ST-TAG          :45
===============================================================================
RAY/SS                                      65 ELEMENTARY SCHOOL TEACHERS WERE
                                            GIVEN SPECIAL AWARDS TODAY.
TAKE TAPE :12                               THE TEACHERS WERE RECOGNIZED FOR USING
super: Today, Harrington :01-:06            INNOVATIVE PROGRAMS THAT MAKE LEARNING
                                            EASIER FOR THEIR STUDENTS.  THE MINI-
                                            GRANTS CAME FROM THE CITY'S JUNIOR
                                            LEAGUE AND ARE BASED ON BOTH TEACHER
                                            CREATIVITY AND STUDENT PARTICIPATION.
TAKE SOUND UP TILL :22
super: Michael Smith, Jr. League of            Outcue.."funds for otherwise."
       Harrington  :14-:18
TAG-RAY/STRAIGHT                            THE GRANTS TOTAL 12-THOUSAND DOLLARS.
                                            THE PROGRAM IS THE FIRST OF ITS KIND
                                            IN THE AREA.
```

FIGURE 3.5. A voice-over/sound bite (VO-bite) script from the newscast outlined in Figure 3.1. The SG# column indicates that the story runs in segment B and is the thirteenth element in the newscast. The CUES listing shows that it starts with the anchor on camera with a graphic or picture (SS), then goes to videotape (TAPE), and winds up with a straight tag (ST-TAG). This script has two supers. The location super (Today, Harrington) is used over the first video, and the identifying super (Michael Smith) is used over the sound bite. The ":12" after the TAKE TAPE command means there are 12 seconds till the sound bite begins. The ".22" after the TAKE SOUND UP TILL command tells the director that the sound bite will begin at 12 seconds into the tape and end at 22 seconds (the sound bite is 10 seconds long). Many newsrooms use this method to indicate the *running times* of tapes. Some directors may prefer to have the script divided into separate tape listings. In that case, TAKE TAPE :12 would remain, but TAKE SOUND UP TILL :22 would probably be replaced by TAKE SOUND BITE—:10. In either case, the tape's total running time would be 22 seconds.

An *incue* consists of the first few words a person says in a sound bite on videotape; an *outcue* comprises the last few words. But an incue can also be a reporter's or anchor's final words leading up to a sound bite or package.

If a reporter is on a live shot and doesn't have time to give the producer a detailed script on the phone, an incue may be used. For example, if a sound bite is being used in the live shot, the reporter can give the producer at least the last three or four words she will be saying before the sound bite starts. That way the producer can let the newscast director know when to switch to the tape with the sound bite; otherwise, viewers will see the reporter finish her remarks and stare either at the camera or a TV monitor, waiting for the videotape to roll. The director, of course, will also have been told the outcue of the sound bite in order to know when to switch back to the reporter on the live shot. (More about what a newscast director does in Chapter 4.)

Package

Stand-up.   A *stand-up* is any shot of a reporter talking to the viewers. You've seen them often on local news and the networks. The stand-up may be at the beginning, end, or middle of a *package*, which is simply a complete story assembled by a reporter. Generally, stand-ups are used at the end of a story, with the reporter summarizing what the story means or mentioning a possible future development. A stand-up at the beginning of a report "sets up" what's coming next.

Bridge.   When a stand-up is used in the middle of a story, it's referred to as a *bridge* because it bridges two elements of a story together. Bridges can be effective tools in helping viewers to better understand a story. For example, let's say a reporter is doing a story on the city council's big fight over buying one of two sites for a new convention center. She starts her story at the city council meeting and then visits the first of the two sites. After reporting on the first site, she appears on camera and says this for the bridge: "But here at the second location being considered, the land is more centrally located. Commissioners seem to favor this location, even though it will cost the city more money." The story then continues with scenes of the second site and anything else pertinent to the report. In this way the reporter bridges together the main elements of the story—those concerning the two convention sites.

The *package*—a complete story done by a reporter—is considered by most to be the backbone of a newscast. It usually consists of video on the story's subject plus interviews with those involved and a stand-up by the reporter, who also narrates the story. The news anchor tells a little about the story to prepare viewers for what they're going to see (the *intro*), followed by something like "Our John Doe has more on the story." At that point the edited story begins, and the anchors aren't seen again until the taped portion of the story concludes. A typical package script is shown in Figure 3.6.

Packages usually have a number of supers. To make sure the director airs them properly, reporters must be very careful about correct super times. Many directors like to have indicated on the script the entire amount of time a super can be aired. Let's say a sound bite is 12 seconds long. If the super time is listed as the first five seconds of the sound bite, the director will not know how much longer that particular sound bite will run in the package. Sometimes directors fall behind and don't put the super on the air right away. If they think they don't have time enough left, they'll just drop it. But if the script indicates the entire "window" in which the sound bite runs, the director will know how much time he's got left to super the person or location.

Tagging out is very important for packages because it makes the anchor an involved party in the story rather than merely its introducer. This is why tags

```
                          PACKAGE SCRIPT
                             ( PKG )


SG#    SLUG                  CUES                     STORY TIME
A 2    WOODS FIRE            RAY/STR/TAPE ST-TAG         1:40
======================================================================
RAY/STRAIGHT                            SOME RIVERTON COUNTY RESIDENTS WERE
                                        CONCERNED THIS MORNING THEY MIGHT LOSE
                                        THEIR HOMES.   THE RECENT DRY WEATHER
                                        WE'VE BEEN HAVING, COMBINED WITH COLD
                                        TEMPERATURES, HAS KILLED OFF A LOT OF
                                        BRUSH.   THIS MORNING IT RESULTED IN A
                                        HUGE GRASS FIRE.   JOHN DAVIS REPORTS
                                        ON SOME ANXIOUS MOMENTS FOR THE GROUP.
TAKE TAPE TILL   1:24
super: Today, Roewood        :01-:05
       Harvey Brown, Roewood Fire Chief
                             :34-:38
       John Davis reporting :42-:46     Outcue: Standard Out
       James Smith, Forest Ranger
                             :52-:58
TAG-RAY/STRAIGHT                        LOCAL FIRE OFFICIALS SAY THEY HAVEN'T
                                        HAD A PROBLEM YET.   HOWEVER, THEY ARE
                                        CONCERNED ABOUT FIRE PROBLEMS NEXT
                                        JANUARY AND FEBRUARY IF THE CURRENT
                                        DRY CONDITIONS PERSIST.
```

FIGURE 3.6. The script for a package, taken from the newscast outlined in Figure 3.1. The script is much like that for a VO-bite, with both location and identifying supers, as well as a straight tag. The words "Standard Out" after the word outcue indicates that the reporter will finish by giving his name and where he is, or the channel number, whichever the news department prefers. For example, he might say "John Davis reporting for Newscenter 5," or "John Davis in Johnson County for Newscenter 5."

should not be throw-away lines; they should be worthwhile additions to the story. This enhances the anchor's credibility (something a station should constantly strive to do). Stories are generally packaged when the subject matter is a little too involved to tell with a VO or VO-bite. But packages are not used only for serious stories; they are used for subjects ranging from violence to humor.

Story Types

Spot news usually refers to stories that break suddenly with no warning, such as fires or bank robberies. But spot news is not always violent. For example, a key city figure decides to announce that she will retire after her current term in office. A news conference is set up, and everyone scrambles down to city hall to get the story.

Hard news is almost always spot news. A bank robbery, murder, or fatal car wreck occurs suddenly, making it spot news. But these stories also involve violence, and many years ago violent news stories were termed hard news. Hard news, however, does not have to be spot news. For instance, a news story about a man on trial for murder involves violence, but the trial is a scheduled event, which removes the story from the spot news category.

A *backgrounder*, as the name implies, is a story about the background of a person, group, object, or place. A backgrounder helps clarify a main story. For example, let's say an old theater is going to be torn down, and the whole episode is causing a lot of controversy, with verbal fights at city council meetings and demonstrations by protest groups. The surrounding controversy is the main story; the backgrounder might focus on the history of the theater, including the big names who appeared there or any notable events that occurred during its lifetime. Played together (controversy first), the two stories will make a well-rounded report.

A *sidebar* is one story done in relation to another—a spin-off of the first. The backgrounder mentioned above is one example, but sidebars are not just backgrounders. Let's say city leaders are trying to decide whether a firm should be allowed to build a sanitary landfill—always a controversial subject (landfills are necessary, but no one wants one near their neighborhood). The main story would be on residents voicing their opposition to the landfill at a city council meeting where a vote is scheduled on the issue.

A sidebar might look at how well the firm has constructed landfills in other places. A reporter and photographer could be sent to a city where the firm has built the same type of landfill it's proposing before the city council. The reporter might talk to area residents about any problems concerning noise, odor, or health. This sidebar could be aired effectively after the main story, or promoted for the next newscast at the conclusion of the main story. Sidebars help viewers better understand complex or controversial stories.

A *series* is a group of stories on a topic of interest to a large number of people. It might involve just two consecutive reports, but could also consist of 10 separate reports run during a two-week period. Most series, however, air for less than a week. Generally, the subject matter is serious in nature, and the reports are run during a ratings period in an effort to draw more viewers. To persuade greater numbers of viewers to tune in, promotion for these stories is often heavier than most other station promotion.

A *documentary* is similar to a series in that it is a relatively lengthy report on a serious subject. Sometimes a station will run a five-to-seven part series and then produce a 30-minute documentary on the same topic to air in a different time period. The typical length is half an hour, but sometimes you'll find hour-long documentaries on local stations. At the network level, the usual length is 60 minutes.

Features are stories that are normally done on lighter subjects and are often (but not always) humorous. Features are packages of about the same length as news stories, but often require especially clever writing. You'll usually see them just before the end of a newscast. They make you laugh, and sometimes make you think.

A *folo* story is one that follows up on the developments of a previous story. The first report may have aired the day, week, month, or even year before. Stories frequently require some type of follow-up at a future date, because something is going to happen at that time to add to or change the story. Let's say a high school student was seriously injured in a cheerleading accident. There would probably be several stories surrounding the accident and the subsequent treatment. But three months later it would be appropriate to do another story on how the student is doing, how much progress she's made, and what's in her immediate future.

Regular viewers like to be updated on stories. It gives them the feeling that the newspeople are on top of things, going beyond the events of just one day. Good reporters keep a list of possible folo stories for slow news days.

Other Important Terms

Editing is a function that every reporter should know and one that virtually all photographers are involved with, except in the very largest markets. It's the process of putting together the best of the videotape shot on a story. Today it's all done electronically (Figure 3.7)—a far cry from the film days, when editing meant cutting film into segments and gluing them together.

Everything that airs must be edited. Only in rare circumstances, such as a late fire, would so-called *raw* (unedited) *tape* be put on the air. If a late-breaking story occurs and there's no time to edit when the crew returns to the station, raw tape may have to be used rather than no tape at all. Someone will have to rewind the raw tape to quickly select something to air. During this process, the tape should be checked to make sure that what airs will be acceptable and not look too rough—that is, full of camera movement as the photographer changed positions for different shots.

In most small-market and many medium-market stations, reporters do their own editing. However, in stations of higher market size, the photographers

FIGURE 3.7. An edit booth, where a reporter edits a story for that night's newscast. The machine on the left plays back the tape shot on the story. The unit on the right records, on another tape, the exact scenes the reporter wants included in the story. The entire editing process is electronic and allows the reporter to preview each edit and make desired changes.

sometimes handle the editing. In the largest markets, the news departments have editors whose sole function is to edit stories. There's generally a union in the latter situation, and the reporter can't even touch an editing machine. This sort of restriction may also be found in some stations whose photographers handle the editing.

A newsroom operates on a *beat system* when it assigns reporters specific areas to cover each day or each week (crime and courts, city or county, medicine, business). The beat system operates best in larger newsrooms where reporters are allowed the necessary time to work their beats and develop stories. In smaller markets most reporters are *general assignment*—they don't specialize. One day they may cover a triple murder, and the next day may find them at a school board meeting. It's difficult to make a beat system work in smaller newsrooms because the reporters are always out getting the day's news and don't have much extra time to make *beat calls* to their contacts.

A *feed* is the transmission of a story to a local station by means of a special telephone line, microwave hookup, or satellite. The transmission is usually of complete stories, but sometimes the feed is simply raw material that a station can edit for its own use. For example, a story can be fed to a station from one of its own live vans for editing at the station. This is sometimes done when the crew at a location is standing by for a live shot and does not have time to physically deliver tapes of previously recorded material to the station. Each day, a station receives feeds from its own network and from many other news sources. Generally, these feeds involve world and national news, but a station might have a special story fed back from Washington on a topic of local interest.

Before the use of satellites, all feeds were transmitted, or *sent*, on a special phone line, or *land line*. But because this line was used to send all network shows, the feeds could only be sent during periods (usually late afternoon or early evening) when the network line was not in use and no program was being sent down. With satellite technology, a number of electronic channels opened up. Networks can now send feeds on one satellite channel while network programming is sent on another channel—perhaps even with a different satellite.

Closed circuit refers to a program or information (not for broadcast) that is sent by a network to its affiliated stations. It may be a program planned for the future or an update on programming information or commercial content on network programs later that day. Until TV satellites came into use, closed circuit information, like any other "feed," could only be sent when programs were not being transmitted by the network for airing. With satellites, however, the network can send its regular programming on one satellite and its closed circuit "feed" on another.

A *TelePrompTer* is a small TV camera mounted over a special moving conveyor belt on which an operator rolls the script of the newscast, page by page. The TV camera actually shoots a picture of each page of the script. This picture is sent out to special monitors mounted on the main studio cameras. The news anchors see the script on these monitors. The TelePrompTer allows them to read news stories while they're looking into the main camera lens.

A *network affiliate* is a station that broadcasts programs provided by one of the TV networks. This is a formal arrangement between the station and the network. The affiliate does broadcast programs of its own in the mid-morning, late afternoon, and early evening, but most of its air time is spent broadcasting network shows.

A station is termed an *independent* if it has no network affiliation. It must program all of its air time, as there are no network shows to fall back on. Independents are mainly found in larger markets, because smaller markets usually don't have enough business to support both network affiliates and independents. However, large cities have a number of independents. Los Angeles, for example, has four very high frequency (VHF) independents on channels 5, 9, 11, and 13 (channel 11 is now a member of the Fox network, which provides limited evening programming, but it still programs most of its day). These stations have news departments that compete with the network affiliates and their local news departments on channels 2, 4, and 7. That's a lot of news.

A *market* is an area served by television stations. A typical market has access to stations representing the three networks, an educational station, and perhaps an independent. Because market size is so important to your future in the business, Chapter 7 is devoted to this subject.

Ratings reflect the viewing preferences of the TV audience. They're taken virtually all the time in the major markets but just four times a year (February, May, July, and November) in most other markets. As you will read in Chapter 8, ratings determine the fate of TV shows and have a big effect on what you see.

Consultants also have a big impact on TV stations everywhere. Failing stations frequently hire consultants to find out what's wrong with their programming and promotion and to come up with plans to fix the problems. You will learn more about consultants in Chapter 9.

Cut-ins are the abbreviated early-morning newscasts that most network affiliates present each day, generally at 7:25 and 8:25 A.M. The network makes a five-minute period available at each of these times so their affiliates can *cut away* from their regular programming to do a local newscast. It's called a cut in because the newscast temporarily interrupts, or cuts into, the network show. If something happens at the local affiliate to prevent the newscast, the local station merely stays with the network programming rather than taking the scheduled cut-in.

News teases are 10- to 30-second announcements, usually made by news anchors, that advertise what's coming up that night on the local newscasts. News teases are frequently run in the late afternoon hours before the 6 P.M. news, and again in the early evening hours prior to the late news. It's simply another way to attract viewers to the newscasts.

You'll hear other expressions, but these are some of the basic ones you need to know. They may vary slightly from newsroom to newsroom, but the meaning is the same.

4 TV News Jobs

Most people don't realize how many jobs are found in a typical TV newsroom. As you might expect, people within the news department have a great deal of interaction with each other but not too much with other individuals at the station. The main exception is the news director, who meets with the general manager and other department heads on a regular basis. Most of the news staff are busy with various projects and don't interface much with anyone other than the production staff that help air the news each day. Let's take a look at the various positions and get an idea of what they involve.

Anchor

We've all watched both local and network news anchors deliver the news on television (Figure 4.1). That half hour is probably the easiest part of their day. Local news anchors generally arrive at the station by 2 P.M. to get ready for that evening's newscast. Most anchors help write scripts for the newscasts, as well as write and anchor the afternoon and evening news teases you see in regular afternoon programming before the early news and again in the evening hours prior to the late news. Anchors will often also do live reports from the scene of a news story or go *on assignment* out of town to cover a special event.

In the vast majority of TV news departments, anchors do their share of work, and it's usually far more than the viewing public realizes. The smaller the market is, the more responsibility the anchor has. In many medium markets and virtually all the smaller markets, news anchors both write and produce the newscasts. This may include some tape editing from time to time. In these markets an anchor may also be the news director and serve as assignment editor as well. In the larger markets, however, anchors can concentrate on helping write the newscasts. As a general rule, the larger the market, the more limited the anchor's responsibilities.

FIGURE 4.1. The four people the public most closely associates with a TV station—its main anchors for the 6 P.M. and 10 or 11 P.M. newscasts. Many people think all the anchors do is show up for work and read news on the set. But most of them work very hard prior to each newscast, which is the culmination of their work.

News anchors are also involved in promotional activities for their stations because they're the most recognizable local personalities the station has. Anchors speak before civic groups, appear on telethons, and take part in many other activities that show their involvement with the community. An anchor almost always comes from the reporting ranks and may have held other jobs in the newsroom, but reporting was the key that opened the door to anchoring (Figure 4.2).

Weathercaster

A station's weathercaster is almost as readily recognizable to the public as the news anchors. Although weathercasters have much less time on the air, they

FIGURE 4.2. A TV news anchor scans AP and UPI wires on his computer screen before writing a story. A newsroom computer system like this eliminates the need for the anchor to travel between his desk and a wire-service machine, because the wires go directly to the computer.

make a big impression on people. As consultants will tell you, viewer interest in weather is very high (Figure 4.3).

During the 1950s and 1960s weathercasters came from all kinds of backgrounds; some had been radio disc jockeys, others TV announcers. But by the late seventies many stations had opted for a weatherperson who was actually trained in weather. This trend has progressed to the point that many big-market weatherpeople today are meteorologists or climatologists. This is true even at a number of medium-market stations.

You'll generally find two weatherpeople at a station—one for the regular Monday-through-Friday newscasts and the other for weekends. The weekend weathercaster will probably do environmental reports for three days during the week; these are included in the newscast like any other report. In some smaller markets, the weekend weathercaster may be a part-time employee.

FIGURE 4.3. A weatherman checks one of his most important pieces of equipment —the weather radar unit. He can choose a radar view ranging from a 25 mile radius to several hundred miles, depending on the weather systems he wants to show in the weathercast seen by viewers at home. This radar unit is located in the studio, near the news set, so any necessary adjustments can be made quickly.

Sportscaster

Sportscasters have backgrounds similar to those of news anchors but deal with sports. They must have the same writing and reporting skills as news anchors; in fact, most sportscasters were news or sports reporters before they moved on to the anchor desk. Many sportscasters today have journalism degrees but were attracted to sports coverage rather than news reporting.

As with weathercasters, you'll usually find two sports anchors at a station, one for the Monday-through-Friday newscasts and one for weekends. The weekend sports anchor generally does sports reporting three days a week. At smaller-market stations, however, the weekend sports anchor may also be pressed into service to cover news stories during the week. This person may even be a part-time employee, like the weekend weathercaster.

News Director

The news director is the head of the news department. In smaller markets this person may also double as the anchor or co-anchor. A news director has usually been a reporter, and probably also a producer and/or assignment editor, at one time or another. The news director has charge of the entire news operation and is responsible for everything that airs during the newscasts except commercials. The general manager of the station usually works closely with the news director on the overall news effort. In larger markets this includes news specials and documentaries that run outside the time periods of the station's newscasts.

A news director who also anchors has a heavy load to carry. This combination of responsibilities is enough to produce a gigantic headache on many days, but the news director in a smaller market may additionally act as assignment editor. In the smallest markets, the news director may also produce the newscasts!

A news director has certain administrative duties, such as budgeting and conducting staff meetings. And we can't forget that new people have to be found and hired when someone resigns; this is also the news director's responsibility. There's always plenty of movement in the smaller markets as young reporters come into a station, get their experience, and move on to bigger and greener pastures. The news director is faced with a constant "revolving door" in the newsroom—just when a new reporter is trained, someone else is saying goodbye, heading to their next job.

A station in a small market simply makes less money than those in bigger markets. It has fewer dollars to put into its news operation, which means a smaller staff with most people doing more than one job (this is usually where you'll find the news director also serving as the anchor). But as long as the station's news staff isn't substantially smaller than that of the other stations in the market, its news department can at least compete. Stations that reach the larger markets have greater revenues (and, presumably, are more profitable) and can thus afford to spend a great deal of money on their news operations. Each market needs a minimum amount of people and equipment to get the job done. As the markets get larger, the staff and equipment must increase accordingly.

Like all of the other employees, the news director at the station that's way behind the others in town in terms of both staff size and salaries is no doubt overburdened. The news staff is always too small to compete with the other stations, and this leads to morale problems. New staff members arrive with a good attitude but are demoralized when they see the many shortcomings of their station as compared with the competition across town. Salaries at this type of station are usually a good deal lower than the market average.

Assistant News Director

This position is almost always limited to upper-medium and larger markets. Assistant news directors usually handle staff scheduling and other tasks assigned by the news director. They also take charge when the news director is absent. Their backgrounds are virtually the same as news directors' and in most cases they anticipate heading a news department of their own.

Assignment Editor

This is perhaps the most demanding and stressful job in a news department, second only to that of news director. The assignment editor sends out reporters and photographers to cover the day's news and often has to juggle crews in the field, shuttling them from one location to another. Let's say all the station's reporters and photographers are out on stories and a bank robbery occurs. The assignment editor has to decide which of the stories being covered is the most expendable and determine which crew is closest to the bank robbery. The crew that is pulled off a story to go to the breaking news event may not have a chance to get back to their original story. Since no one else is available to cover it, that first story will probably be lost. This constant "people-moving" creates many headaches.

The assignment editor is usually responsible for keeping what are commonly referred to as *future files*. These are files on upcoming stories, with as much information as possible about the event: what, where, when, who to see at the scene for more about the story, phone numbers, and other details. The assignment editor gets this information from various sources, such as

- Phone calls from people wanting coverage of an event
- Mailings to the news department concerning a possible story
- Information about future events clipped from newspapers and other sources
- Police scanners
- Reporters themselves

Police scanners—electronic devices that enable newsrooms to monitor the radio bands used by the police—are an excellent source of hard news such as shootings, wrecks, robberies, and the like, *if* someone is listening to them constantly. They're found in every newsroom. The assignment editor attempts to keep an ear open to the various fire and police calls, and if something happens, a news crew is dispatched to the scene. In many markets the crew consists of a reporter and a photographer (or a photographer alone, if no one else is available). In large markets there may be a reporter, a photographer, and a third person to run the videotape recorder. In the case of networks, a fourth member—a field producer—joins the crew. Field producers do anything, from carrying out interviews for the reporter to performing many other tasks involved in getting the story together and making the reporter look good.

The assignment editor or assistant assignment editor (if the station has one) makes *beat calls* several times a day. He or she telephones various police, fire, government, and court offices to find out what's going on, either that day or on a coming day. In the larger markets, because of bigger staffs, a reporter is generally assigned to a beat, such as the courts, city hall, or fire and police. The reporter is expected to maintain contact with one or more important persons on the beat and to keep the assignment editor informed of possible story ideas. Reporters often run into stories from sources other than their regular beats. They may pick up information for a new story while covering something else. A reporter's contacts (beat or otherwise) can be an extremely good source of stories.

The typical assignment editor could use two heads and four arms to handle the daily workload. Newsrooms in larger markets usually have an assistant assignment editor to help out. Many news departments have a newsroom secretary who takes the load of incoming phone calls off the assignment editor's shoulders. In smaller markets, however, you generally won't find either an assignment editor or assistant assignment editor, so their duties are handled by the news director.

As you can see, the assignment editor is an extremely busy person. He or she may have begun as a reporter, but decided at some point to make a career change and move into the administrative end of the business rather than continue with on-air work. The next step on the career ladder for assignment editor is generally the position of executive producer or assistant news director. Most have the goal of eventually becoming a news director.

Executive Producer

Like the assistant news director, the executive producer is usually found only in larger markets. The executive producer is the general overseer of all the newscasts and has a great deal of input as to which stories are run in each newscast, what the lead story will be, and so forth.

An executive producer usually wants to become a news director. The next possible move up the career ladder for someone in this position is to assistant news director or news director.

Many of the larger-market stations have a newscast at 5 P.M., another at 6, and the final one of the day at 10 or 11 P.M., depending on the time zone. Network programming runs from 7 to 10 P.M. in the Central and Mountain time zones, which means the late newscast starts at 10 o'clock; however, in the Eastern and Pacific zones, the network shows begin at 8 and end at 11, with the late news starting at 11 P.M. A large-market station may have a producer for each of these newscasts, all under the direction of the executive producer.

Producer

The producer is the immediate manager of the newscast. She coordinates the countless details of a clean and professional broadcast, including such tasks as integrating final script lengths, deciding which anchor will read each story, and determing that all the necessary elements for the broadcast are assembled.

The producer meets in the early afternoon with the news director, executive producer (if there is one), assignment editor, and news anchors to go over the news gathered that day. At this time a decision is made as to which story will be the lead, which will be second, and so on. A great many things must be done to get a newscast on the air, and the producer is the one who generally coordinates these details (Figure 4.4).

A producer has usually been a reporter and should therefore be a competent writer; however, in the larger markets, this person deals mainly with "the big picture." Many producers in the smaller markets write part of the newscast, along with the anchors and reporters. In the very smallest markets there may be no producer; the anchor or co-anchors take care of the job. This is certainly not the ideal situation, but in the smaller markets there's just not enough money to support a large staff. Producers generally want to advance to executive producer, assistant news director, and finally news director.

Assistant Producer

This position is one found only in larger news operations. As the title implies, the assistant producer aids the producer in the preparation of the newscast. This person has more authority than the production assistant mentioned later

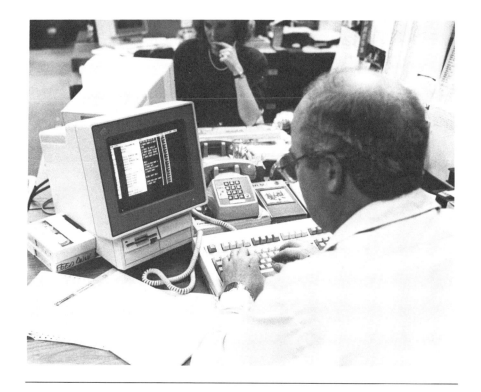

FIGURE 4.4. The computer is a real timesaver for a newscast producer. Many things can be done with a computer that would take a great deal more time if done by hand. The newscast must be timed so that it's not too long or too short. This is one of many jobs the computer automatically does for the producer.

in the chapter. Sometimes the titles are used interchangeably, but they really shouldn't be. For instance, an assistant producer may have editorial control over part of the newscast, whereas a production assistant rarely has such authority.

Reporter

Reporters usually want to become anchors because of the higher pay, greater authority, and prestige. Many anchors began as reporters, but there are exceptions; some older anchors on the air today came out of radio and went straight into TV anchoring.

As you know, reporters go into the field with photographers to gather the news (the exception to this, the *one-man band*, is covered later). Generally, the assignment editor sends reporters to stories from various sources (as mentioned earlier, reporters in the larger markets are assigned to specific beats).

Before leaving the station the reporter discusses the story with the assignment editor, as well as what form it might take—VO, sound bite, VO-bite, or package. Of course, when the reporter arrives at the scene, things may have changed; something entirely different or even more important may be going on. In this case the reporter would inform the assignment editor of the latest developments. The producer would also be told as soon as possible. Depending on how important the story is, the producer may want to run it in a different location in that night's newscast.

Earlier, in referring to the typical two-person team of reporter and photographer, an exception was mentioned—the so-called one-man band, a reporter who is also trained to be a photographer. One-man bands are found in the smallest markets, and sometimes the not-so-small ones, where the budget isn't big enough to support separate reporters and photographers. This overworked individual needs reporting and photography skills, as well as more than 40 pounds of video gear, to tackle an assignment. Arriving at the scene, he or she must not only cover the story as a reporter but also shoot it as a photographer—not an easy task.

Pretend you're a one-man band. While taking notes, you may be missing some good video; while shooting video, information important to the story could be lost. Interviewing people is difficult because you have to talk to them *and* photograph them. Obviously, there's no way one person can do the job of two and still come out with a top-notch product. Anyone who has done one-man-band work will tell you that both the photography and reporting suffered.

This is why a two-person team of reporter and photographer is best. Unfortunately, budgetary constraints in the smallest markets often make one-man bands necessary. Because of the strenuousness of the job and the limitations it places on the quality of one's work, most reporters do not want to work as a one-man band for very long. Many take such a position because it is all they can get. After a year or so on the job, however, they will have gained enough experience to move on to larger markets where stations have separate reporters and photographers.

Reporters who specialize—such as medical, economic, business, or feature reporters—usually work in the larger markets, where stations can afford specialists. But most reporters are *general assignment* reporters. They might cover a fire one day and a groundbreaking for a new civic center the next. Consequently, they must be adaptable and certainly need thick skins at times. Most good reporters have covered all kinds of stories in their careers. And the specialists almost always began as general assignment reporters, probably working in that capacity for several years or more.

Most reporters want to anchor one day. But what if the reporter is really not cut out for anchoring, yet doesn't want to remain a reporter? If that's the case, a reporter who loves the business may decide to move into the administrative or management side of news. This might mean becoming an assignment editor, producer, executive producer, or news director. If none of these options are appealing, another choice might be radio journalism. The possibilities are discussed in the final chapter, "Career Changes and Alternatives."

Photographer

The photographer—sometimes called a *shooter*—is the important other half of the typical two-person news team. Now that videotape has widely replaced film, the photographer is sometimes formally referred to as a *videographer*. In most cases, however, you'll still find *photographer* being used (not to be confused with *still photographer*). When a story happens, if there's something to shoot—any video possibilities at all—you can do without a reporter but not without a photographer.

Photographers must haul a lot of weight around, and this sometimes gets in the way of shooting the story. Back in the days of film, camera equipment wasn't so heavy and bulky; as videotape equipment arrived on the scene, a lot of weight came with it. In the mid-seventies the gear in common use weighed more than 40 pounds, counting the camera, recorder, batteries, and other miscellaneous items—a heavy load for a photographer who had far to walk or run. The more recent generations of videotape equipment have greatly reduced the size and weight of portable video, but a photographer's gear remains considerable (Figure 4.5).

Experienced photographers usually have very good ideas about stories and how they should be shot. Well-trained reporters know this and collaborate with photographers on their stories. Working as a team, they will produce consistently better stories than reporters and photographers who don't work closely together. A reporter will tell the photographer the specifics she wants, based on her vision of the story—for example, shots of a particular person. But a photographer should know in general what video is necessary and get those shots while the reporter gathers information about the story.

As mentioned in Chapter 3, photographers generally do a certain amount of videotape editing. This is true in all but the biggest markets, where stations have editors who handle that chore. At some stations the reporters do the lion's share of editing, while at others the photographers have that responsibility.

Many photographers have journalism degrees, even though they ultimately turned to photography. Some colleges offer majors in photojournalism or cine-

FIGURE 4.5. In Figure 2.1 you saw all the videotape gear the average TV photographer has to carry. Well, here it is, all loaded on the photographer, except for the tripod. You can see why most TV photographers are tired at the end of the day!

matography, but most don't. A number of today's photographers previously worked in other capacities in TV stations and were able to spend time with news photographers to learn the business. Then, when an opening occurred in the newsroom, they jumped right in.

Production Assistant

In some cases, the assistant to a producer is called a production assistant rather than an assistant producer. That's because the position involves a lot of miscellaneous tasks around the newsroom but no editorial decisions such as those made by producers and assistant producers. The production assistant might be loading paper in a news printer one minute and editing videotape the next.

Large- and medium-market stations have production assistants, but the smaller markets can't afford them. Instead, the job is handled by anyone free at the time—a reporter, photographer, or intern, if one is available.

Video Archivist

As you can imagine, many stations shoot a vast amount of videotape and air many stories each month. For legal purposes, these stories have to be saved for at least one year; however, most newsrooms keep them much longer than that—sometimes for 10 years or more. The main objective is to have available a big video library of background footage for stories. A simple example of a story in which such footage might be used is a report on an upcoming murder trial. Let's say the murder took place a year and a half ago. The reporter putting the story together will undoubtedly want to use some footage of the murder scene shot when the murder was initially covered. This helps viewers understand the story better by recalling when and where the murder took place.

A video archivist is in charge of researching and retrieving the needed footage. This job is unlikely to exist in many medium-market and all small-market stations because of budgetary restraints. In such stations, the news director or some other capable person is responsible for keeping the archives up to date. In the larger markets (with their longer newscasts), so many stories are shot and aired that this becomes a full-time job.

A video archivist watches over the video library, adds each day's stories to it, and keeps a complete record of it (most likely on computer). The archivist often has other recordkeeping duties as well.

Newscast Director

Even though this position sounds similar to that of news director, the two should not be confused. The newscast director is the person responsible for guiding the technical aspects of the newscast from beginning to end. In many markets, the newscast director actually switches cameras, pushes buttons to roll videotape, and handles much of the electronic end of getting a newscast on the air. This person also gives anchors instructions and directs camera operators and others while the newscast is underway.

In other markets, however, this job is divided in half, with two people doing the work. In such cases, the newscast director generally does not operate any equipment (except perhaps the character generator) but is in charge of the operation and determines the camera shots. The camera-switching and much of the technical work are handled by a technical director. In a reasonably sophisticated newscast, this arrangement is best, because two people can handle the job better than one.

This chapter has outlined the most common positions in a newsroom. Even though the titles may vary from station to station, the staff will be carrying out similar duties. Additional jobs will generally be found in the larger markets where more money is available to spend on bigger staffs.

Remember: in the largest markets you'll find many more jobs and specialists. In the smallest markets there are fewer jobs and no specialists; one person may be doing more than one job. It's the nature of the business.

5 Newsroom Organization

The job descriptions in Chapter 4 outline what people in various newsroom positions do. Now we'll see how some typical news departments are staffed.

A Basic News Operation

For our first example, let's assume a newsroom with 21 full-time people plus one part-time weekend weatherperson, as shown in Figure 5.1. You might find a staff of this size in small- to medium-sized markets. This is a fairly solid organization that can cover a range of stories with reasonable quality and sophistication. Each of the primary responsibilities for the production is covered by only one person; no one wears more than one hat. This obviously allows personnel to focus more intently and therefore to do a better job. Later you'll see how a newsroom can be pared down to just the essentials in the smallest markets.

Staff Breakdown

The personnel in a newsroom of this size might have the following responsibilities:

News director. The news director arrives at the newsroom between 8 and 9 A.M. He handles most of the administrative duties and manages the entire news operation (the assignment editor may help with smaller problems); he has no anchoring responsibilities. Since staff turnover is fairly high, the news director needs to keep on the lookout for qualified job applicants. Because the staff is relatively small, a resignation can hurt the whole news-gathering effort until a replacement is on the job. Consequently, the news director must spend a certain amount of time viewing audition (résumé) tapes from applicants.

Either the news director or the assignment editor is in the newsroom at all times, if possible. This is especially critical in the late morning to early afternoon hours, when all the crews are generally out. Because there's no newsroom secretary, the news director and the assignment editor are the only staff available to listen to the police scanners and answer the phones.

Every day around 2:30 P.M., the news director holds an editorial meeting with the assignment editor, producer, and both news anchors. During this meeting they discuss the stories covered that day and the order in which they should run in the night's newscast.

Throughout the day, as the reporters write their stories, either the news director, assignment editor, or producer checks the reporters' copy. With at least these three staff members assigned to the process, there will always be someone on hand, day or night, to copyedit reporters' stories. The editing process is designed to catch factual errors and bad grammar as well as to ensure proper script format.

Assignment editor.   The assignment editor is usually in by 7:30 in the morning to check the AP and UPI wire services. She makes some beat calls (if these have not already been made by the morning cut-in anchor/reporter) to see if anything happened overnight that may require an immediate follow-up. The assignment editor works closely with the news director in making decisions throughout the day.

Producer.   He produces both the 6 P.M. and the late news. The producer arrives by 2 P.M. to check wires and stories already written that day and to get ready for the editorial meeting. The producer also assists with the phones and listens to the police scanners, especially at night.

News co-anchors (two).   They arrive by 2 P.M. for the editorial meeting. Besides helping to write the newscasts in our 21-person newsroom, they also write stories shot by photographers when no reporter was available. In addition, they keep an ear to the police scanners and help with the phones.

Weather anchor.   The weatherperson comes in by 2 P.M., like the other anchors.

Weekday sports anchor.   This person, who is also the sports director, is generally in by two o'clock, but may arrive earlier to go out on an early sports story. The weekday sports anchor usually heads a two-person operation that includes the weekend sports anchor/reporter.

Weekend sports anchor.   She anchors the weekend sports and sits in for the sports director during the week as needed. The weekend sports anchor also works three weekdays as a sports reporter during either the day or evening shift, depending on what sports stories need to be covered.

Reporters (six).   This is a small reporting staff to adequately cover two shifts from 8 A.M. till 11 P.M., but it can still be managed. Some reporters also handle weekend anchoring duties.

This station, like most, has morning newscasts, so one of the reporters (#1) must come in no later than 5 A.M. This morning reporter is usually assigned to the earliest story possible after the newscasts in order to cover the story, return to the station, and edit it in time to leave around two o'clock (remember, this reporter's day starts at 5 A.M.).

Another reporter (#6) is assigned night-reporting duties. This person may do special reports for the late news but, because of the small staff, will probably have to cover something for the 6 P.M. news as well. The night reporter arrives at the newsroom by 2 P.M.

The morning and night reporters are the only two who work Monday through Friday; the other four do anchoring and reporting on various combinations of weekdays and weekend days.

In Figure 5.1 you'll see that reporter #2 works Tuesday through Saturday, and reporter #3 handles the Sunday-through-Thursday shift. This way, one of them works the day shift on Saturday and the other on Sunday. (In many cases you'll find only one reporter and photographer working the day shift on weekends. It's not ideal, but weekends are usually slow, and one team can probably take care of covering the day's news.) They will be helped by a night photographer who comes in around 2 P.M.

Reporters #4 and #5 each work on Saturday and Sunday plus three weekdays. These two are the co-anchors and producers of the weekend news as well as reporters for three weekdays. On weekends, these co-anchors must help write anything that's not written by the day reporter. Sometimes one of them goes out on night assignments between the two evening newscasts because no reporter is assigned to weekend nights. You'll notice one anchor/reporter (#4) works Saturday through Wednesday, while the other (#5) is scheduled for Wednesday through Sunday. This ensures that both are not off on the same days during the week, leaving the reporting staff seriously low.

As Figure 5.1 shows, a total of three daytime reporters (including the morning reporter) are scheduled for Monday and Friday, four for Tuesday and Thursday, and five for Wednesday. Obviously, personnel schedules must be carefully managed. If, for example, both weekend anchors were off on Monday and Tuesday, the reporting staff would consist of only two daytime reporters on Monday. If one of these reporters were sick, the newsroom would be in serious trouble.

Photographers (seven).   One is the chief photographer (#1) and works weekdays with morning reporter #1. Photographers #2 through #6 have schedules that roughly match those of the other reporters. Photographer #7 helps out three nights during the week and both weekend evenings. This gives the weekend crew someone to shoot video at night, if needed. Photographer #7 may also assist the sports reporter on assignments.

The chief photographer has to keep up with advances in photographers' gear and work with the news director on ordering new equipment or parts. Because he is assigned to work with the morning reporter, he will be able to return to the station in time to take care of these duties on most days.

Weekend weather anchor. This job can usually be filled by a part-time person, so many stations hire a radio announcer who looks and sounds good on TV. With a fairly small amount of training, most such announcers can do an acceptable job.

As noted earlier, this staff of 21 (plus one part-time employee) includes no one to handle the phones. That becomes the responsibility of the news director and assignment editor, along with any reporters or photographers who happen to be available. In a small department (and this is by no means the smallest), everyone pitches in to help. Figure 5.1 shows that the staff is largest on Wednesday; all five day reporters are in, as well as the night reporter. This makes Wednesday a good day to work on special reports. For example, four reporters can cover the day's news while the fifth is assigned to a series.

You'll also see that the staff is smallest on the weekends. In an already small news department, the reporters and photographers must be used where they'll do the most good, and that's on weekdays. Besides, as mentioned, weekends are frequently slow, so a small staff can usually handle the volume.

Because of the reduced activity on many weekends, the anchors may be faced with the problem of not having enough local stories to fill out the newscast. To help the situation, special features and other stories can be stockpiled from the week's closed-circuit network feed of stories. Many stations also subscribe to companies that supply a wide variety of prepackaged stories sent by either videotape or daily satellite. Of course, newscasts should not just be "filled." Each story aired should have some interest and possible relevance to the station's audience.

Where Do You Fit In?

If you're looking for your first job, where do you fit into this newsroom? Assuming you're a reporter, you will most likely be put into one of the strictly reporting slots (reporter #4 or #5). You don't have the experience to do the morning cut-ins, so you probably won't be considered for that job yet. Needless to say, you won't be considered qualified for the position of weekend anchor/

```
                          21-PERSON NEWS STAFF
                          (plus one part-time)


     SUNDAY  *   MONDAY  * TUESDAY * WEDNESDAY * THURSDAY *  FRIDAY  * SATURDAY
     ----------------------------------------------------------------------------

      Off     |======== Morning Reporter #1 & Chief Photog #1 =======|   Off
                         (cut-in anchor)

      Off     |================= Assignment Editor ==================|   Off


      Off     |=================== News Director ====================|   Off


      Off          Off     |=============== Reporter #2 & Photog #2 ===========|


   |============== Reporter #3 & Photog #3 ============|    Off       Off


   |===== Reporter #4 & Photog #4 ==========|   Off        Off     |=========|
              (weekend co-anchor)

   |=======|    Off        Off     |======== Reporter #5 & Photog #5 =========|
                                             (weekend co-anchor)

      Off     |====================== Producer =====================|   Off


      Off     |==================== News Co-Anchor =================|   Off


      Off     |==================== News Co-Anchor =================|   Off


      Off     |==================== Weather Anchor =================|   Off


      Off     |==================== Sports  Anchor =================|   Off


      Off     |========== Night Reporter  #6  & Photog #6 ===========|   Off


   |=======|    Off        Off     |======= Sports Reporter & Photog # 7 ======|


   |=======|   Weekend Weather Anchor (part-time, weekends only)   |=========|
```

FIGURE 5.1.   Chart of the personnel and weekly schedules of a basic 21-member news staff.

reporter—that would come only after a little anchoring experience, such as doing the morning cut-ins. And you probably won't be given the night reporting job. If the station has live-shot capability, the night reporter will be called on from time to time to do live shots in both the six o'clock and late newscasts— not a job for a beginner. However, there are exceptions to the rule. If you have a pleasant voice, good appearance, and present yourself well on camera, you might be able to start as the morning reporter/cut-in anchor in a very small market.

A reporter who has had some experience doing morning cut-ins will usually be considered for a weekend anchor position, should one become available. A weekend anchor may have a chance at a main anchor job if there's an opening. So keep your eyes open and be ready for any possibility!

A Minimal News Operation

How can we cut the staff even more and still get the news on the air? Well, it can be done, although quality always suffers when one person wears two or three hats. Here's an example of a staff cut to the bone (Figure 5.2). There are seven full-time and two part-time employees.

News director/producer/anchor/assignment editor. This person arrives at the station by 1 or 2 P.M. Besides being news director, he is also the single anchor, producer and assignment editor. This means that he must plan the next day's coverage before the night is over, leaving specific directions for the small daytime reporting staff. During the morning and early afternoon when the staff is out, the phones may go unanswered. The police scanners will have to be monitored by reporters, either in the news vehicles or the newsroom, de- pending on the reporters' locations. It's a bad situation, but there's no other choice—the news director can't be expected to arrive at 9 A.M. and stay until nearly midnight each day.

Sports director. This person anchors the weekday sportscasts and does all the sports reporting. On this small staff, weekend sports is handled by a part-timer, so the sports director has no help during the week.

Weather anchor. At a station with a news department this small, the weath- erperson probably has little of the new equipment available to present the weather.

Reporters (four). It's almost impossible to make do with fewer than four reporters, taking weekends and occasional illnesses into consideration. In this newsroom, all the reporters are one-man bands who do their own shooting.

```
                      7-PERSON NEWS STAFF
                      (plus two part-timers)


  SUNDAY *  MONDAY  * TUESDAY * WEDNESDAY * THURSDAY *  FRIDAY  * SATURDAY
  ---------------------------------------------------------------------------

    Off     |================ Morning Reporter #1 ================|    Off
                            (cut-in anchor)

    Off     |=========== News Director/Anchor/Producer ===========|    Off
                          & Assignment Editor

  |=======|      Off        Off     |=============== Reporter #2 ===============|
                                            (weekend anchor)

  |============= Reporter #3 ==============|    Off        Off     |=========|
        (fill-in weekend or morning anchor)

        |=================== Weather Anchor =================|    Off


    Off   |==================== Sports  Anchor =================|    Off


    Off   |================== Night Reporter #4 ================|    Off
                  (possible fill-in weekend or morning anchor)

  |=======|      Weekend Sports Anchor  (part-time only)       |=========|
                    (fill-in weekday sports anchor)

  |=======|      Weekend Weather Anchor (part-time only)       |=========|
                  (possible fill-in weekday weather anchor)
```

FIGURE 5.2. Chart of the personnel and weekly schedules of a minimal seven-member news staff.

Reporter #1 produces and anchors the morning cut-ins and then reports. Reporter #2 is a daytime reporter Wednesday through Friday and serves as the weekend anchor. Reporter #3 works Saturday through Wednesday as a daytime reporter, and reporter #4 is scheduled for weeknights.

Weekend weather anchor.   This is a part-time person, usually a local radio announcer. The job might even be filled by a student who does well on camera.

Weekend sports anchor.   This part-time position is filled by someone with a background similar to that of the weekend weather anchor.

As you can see, this staff of seven (plus two part-timers) is a bare-bones crew! You may wonder who covers weekend nights. Well, if something serious happens, the weekend anchor contacts one of the four reporters (generally, they are on call for weekend nights on a rotating basis). Actually, the newsroom staff could be cut to six people by eliminating the weeknight reporter and making that an on-call position too.

Since the news director at this station is also handling the jobs of producer, anchor, and assignment editor, someone must help out during the morning hours before he comes in. A good choice would be the morning cut-in anchor/reporter, who arrives early anyway. After the cut-ins, the reporter could make changes to the day's assignments, based on what has happened that morning.

Everyone in a small news department like this has to really pitch in to get each day's job done. Keep in mind that you may have to begin your career in such a station. In a news department of this size, you would most likely be a reporter/photographer one-man band. But handling both jobs is difficult at best, and most people won't want to do it for a great length of time. The work itself isn't bad for the entry-level newsperson, who is still in a learning period. After some experience, you'll be good enough to advance to a larger market. Then you can specialize in your primary interest, reporting or photography.

Larger Newsrooms

Let's assume we're in a market that's a little larger, where staff can be added to do a more thorough job of covering the news as well as airing important series and other special reports. We'll return to our staff of 21 plus a part-time weatherperson and build from there. Here are some needed additions:

Newsroom secretary. This addition would be an enormous help to the news director and the assignment editor because both of them would no longer be tied down to the newsroom. The secretary could field calls, take messages, and handle many miscellaneous jobs to free up other staff members. Duties would possibly include the computer archiving of stories (in larger markets this is often such a big job that someone must be hired to do this alone).

Additional reporter and photographer. This would perhaps allow the station to broadcast a regular medical segment or some other type of special report. Most larger stations opt for a medical report at least every other day. Medical segments always show up as high-interest items in consultants' surveys, which is why you'll see them on most of the better stations.

Assistant producer. Works with the producer on the same shift. This would relieve the producer of some minor chores and allow her to concentrate on ways to improve the newscast.

Weekend producer. Produces weekend newscasts and acts as assistant producer on three weekdays. This person would take a big load off the weekend anchors. As a result, the newscasts would look more professional and less harried.

With these additions, the total staff consists of 26 full-time people and one part-timer. From here on, logical additions would be more reporters and photographers. A staff of only 30 can begin to do a good job of covering the news in a medium market and also add some special features.

Should you ever be in a large-market newsroom in a city like New York, Chicago, or Los Angeles, you'll see a staff of close to 100 (perhaps even more). A newsroom of this size will have substantially more reporters and photographers, but there will also be additional back-up personnel such as assistant producers, production assistants, and researchers. The quality, scope, and sophistication of large-market newscasts usually demand these larger staffs. Also, many of the big markets have long early newscasts that run from 4 P.M. to 6:30; with so much news to put together, a large staff is essential. But keep in mind that this expanded newsroom is paid for with the revenue obtained from commercials seen by an audience much larger than that in a small market. It costs sponsors a great deal more money to run commercials in the big cities than elsewhere, so large-market stations have additional income to devote to their news operation. The stakes are higher in larger markets: the potential audience is greater, the revenues are higher, there is more news to cover, and the audience has come to expect higher-quality coverage than in a small market.

It must be emphasized that the staffing examples used in this chapter are more than just examples; they reflect actual staffing in many newsrooms around the country. Almost always, the newsroom with the smallest staff in a market is in third place in the news ratings and will probably always be there, unless new owners take over and infuse some money (as well as promotion) into the news department. But remember—although a third-place station may not be the best place to work, it's where you just might get your first opportunity.

6   A Typical Newsroom Day

Let's take an average day in the newsroom and follow it from beginning to end. You'll notice many of the decisions that have to be made as the day unfolds, how the six o'clock newscast is put together, and the reasons for running stories in a particular order. I'll also explain why some stories are rewritten and used for the late news (10 or 11 P.M.) and why others are discarded completely. We'll assume this newsroom has a 21-person staff like the one outlined in Chapter 5.

Let's say it's Monday. Reporters #2 and #5 are off today, leaving us with the morning reporter (#1) and reporters #3 and #4. The night reporter (#6) is scheduled to come to work at 2 P.M.

At most stations the staff is small in the early morning hours. For that reason, the morning reporter operates virtually alone in the preparation of the morning newscasts. Because there is usually no one to help edit stories or to check scripts for possible mistakes or other problems, the reporter must be especially careful in writing stories. Also, there is no newscast director in the early morning; this person's tasks usually are handled by the morning technical director. This is possible because the morning newscasts are five minutes or less in length and are never as complicated as a full half-hour newscast.

5 A.M.   The morning reporter (#1) arrives at the newsroom. She first checks the wires to see what local or regional stories can be used in the two morning newscasts (cut-ins) at 7:25 and 8:25.

5:20 A.M.   She makes beat calls to local police and fire departments to see if anything major has happened during the night. During one call she learns of a drug bust that occurred shortly after 2 A.M. County police didn't want anyone to know about the bust ahead of time for fear the suspects would get word, so no one in the newsroom was phoned (some police agencies have a public relations person who calls the news departments; most, however, do not).

Morning beat calls occasionally provide a new story (in today's case, the drug bust), or supply information for an update of a story that aired the previous night at 11.

5:35 A.M. Beat calls are over. Reporter #1 has enough information on the drug bust to do a reader for the upcoming newscasts. If time permits, an updated version may be written for the 8:25 A.M. cut-in.

5:50 A.M. She goes over last night's 11 o'clock scripts to see what new stories aired that weren't seen earlier on the 6 P.M. newscast. It's best to use as much news as possible that was fresh at 11 P.M. so the cut-ins don't appear to be a mere rehash of the previous day's 6 P.M. news. But major stories from the day before (regardless of when they aired) should be updated if possible and used in the cut-ins.

6:10 A.M. After going over the scripts, reporter #1 rewrites everything needed for the first cut-in at 7:25. Because there are less than 50 minutes between the cut-ins, she also writes as much of the second one as possible.

6:50 A.M. With the scripts written for the 7:25 cut-in, she goes to the edit booth to re-edit the tapes needed, depending on how she rewrote the stories (that is, as VOs, VO-bites, etc.). Sometimes a tape used at 11 P.M. for a VO or VO-bite can be used again "as is."

7:15 A.M. There's just enough time to put on TV makeup and get scripts to the technical director before the 7:25 newscast.

7:25 A.M. The first cut-in begins and goes relatively smoothly, considering all the work reporter #1 has had to do—check wires and 11 P.M. scripts, rewrite and edit stories, make beat calls, and answer the phone.

7:30 A.M. The first cut-in is over, but this is no time to relax. The rest of the second cut-in needs to be written.

7:35 A.M. The assignment editor arrives and checks with reporter #1 on what has transpired so far this morning. The reporter tells him about the drug bust she learned of while making beat calls. The assignment editor then checks the wires for any new area or local stories that may need to be followed up today.

7:55 A.M. The morning reporter finishes writing scripts for the second cut-in and goes to the edit booth again to re-edit two stories.

8:05 A.M. The assignment editor makes more beat calls. He finds out that the marijuana confiscated in the 2 A.M. drug bust will be burned this morning at 10 o'clock at the county landfill. He includes this in the day's list of stories to be covered.

8:15 A.M. The morning reporter finishes editing, gets the scripts to the director, and checks her TV makeup prior to the cut-in.

8:25 A.M. The second cut-in goes a little smoother than the first. She's not as harried for this newscast. There's been an opportunity to arrive on the set a few minutes before the broadcast to check over her scripts.

8:30 A.M. The second cut-in is over. The assignment editor sends the morning reporter to her first story of the day. A new school is to be dedicated, not too far from the station. The story is expected to be a VO-bite. There will be video of the new school and the crowds, plus a sound bite with the new principal. Reporter #1 leaves with the chief photographer, who had arrived a little earlier and is ready to go.

8:35 A.M. The news director arrives. She and the assignment editor meet briefly to review the news coverage as planned for the day so far (Figure 6.1). This is usually written on a large *assignment board* located in a prominent place in the newsroom. The assignment board shows the time of each story, what it's called, what form it's expected to take (e.g., VO, VO-bite, package), and which news crew will cover it. The board shows only the stories the assignment editor knows about prior to 9 A.M. If there are any changes, he will update the board as the day progresses. The assignment editor brings the news director up to date on the drug bust and tells her that a crew will be covering the drug burn later that morning.

8:40 A.M. Reporter #3 arrives to go out on a city council story that begins at nine o'clock. The main issue is a zoning request that residents plan to oppose heavily. This story is expected to be a package because of its controversial nature and the number of people opposing the zoning request. Photographer #3 has already loaded the necessary equipment and is ready to leave.

8:45 A.M. With beat calls and other checks over, the assignment editor begins to go over the morning mail for possible assignments. He finds a press release about a blood drive that will be kicked off that afternoon at 2:30 (sometimes people in charge of mailing out press releases don't do it early enough; this one should have been received last Friday).

9:30 A.M. Reporter #4 arrives. He's on a schedule that calls for him to come in a little later than the other reporters and stay until 6:30 P.M. Frequently, reporters' hours are staggered, with some coming in later than others. This ensures that a reporter or two are in the newsroom past the 6 P.M. news so they can help out with writing and editing, if needed, once their own stories are finished. The assignment editor sends reporter #4 and his photographer to cover the burning of the marijuana taken in the drug bust. It's scheduled

TIME	STORY (Slug)	TYPE	CREW
8:45am	New School	VO-bite	Reporter/Photog #1
9:00am	City Council (Zoning)	Package	Reporter/Photog #3
10:00am	Drug Burn	VO-bite	Reporter/Photog #4
10:30am	County Roads	Package	Reporter/Photog #1
11:00am	Relic Found	Package	Reporter/Photog #4
1:30pm	Fashions	Package	Reporter/Photog #4
2:00pm	Computer	Package	Reporter/Photog #6
2:30pm	Blood Drive	VO-bite	Reporter/Photog #3
7:30pm	Chemicals/Lake (for late news)	Package	Reporter/Photog #6

FIGURE 6.1. The assignment board, which lists stories to be covered during the day. These stories are those the assignment editor has planned to cover as of 9 A.M. Monday. It's important to note that the content of the stories may change, and the type as well (e.g., VO, VO-bite, package), depending on what the reporters come up with. Or the news director and producer may decide to make a story a VO-bite, although originally planned as a package. This sort of decision might be made as late as the editorial meeting that afternoon at 2:30. Then too, other stories might crop up that have to be covered, necessitating changes in the reporters' assignments.

You will notice that reporter #3 and photographer #3 are scheduled for only two stories. That's because the story on the zoning issue is expected to take all morning and possibly run into the afternoon; hundreds of residents plan to pack the meeting and oppose the zoning issue. However, the assignment editor hopes crew #3 can still get to the blood drive at 2:30 and shoot that story quickly without interfering with their zoning story, because the other crews are hard-pressed in the afternoon.

Remember, this is the way the day starts out for the newsroom. As the day progresses, spot news that occurs might change a story from a package to a VO-bite. This can happen if a reporter is pulled off of one story and sent to cover another before shooting enough tape or gathering enough information for the first story.

for 10 A M at the landfill, and 30 minutes is more than enough time to get there. The story will probably be a VO-bite. The video will show the marijuana being laid out and burned, while the sound bite will be a narcotics detective's comments on how much was confiscated, its street value, and any arrests made.

Reporter #4 plans to go right from the marijuana burn to the home of a woman who has found what's believed to be a historic relic in her backyard.

The assignment editor had called her yesterday and set up a time to shoot the story. It was agreed that 11 A.M. or a little later would be convenient.

9:45 A.M. The morning reporter (#1) returns from covering the story on the new school and checks her videotape. It's very important to be certain that anything shot earlier came out well. All kinds of things can and do go wrong with videotape recorders and cameras, so it's wise to look at your tapes as soon as possible to make sure you've got the story. If not, you may be able to go back and get the interview you've lost, or at least some sort of replacement material. Many a package has been lost because of equipment failure, and all the reporter could do was turn the story into a VO.

9:55 A.M. The tapes have been quickly checked; there's no problem. The morning reporter then meets with the assignment editor about her next story. It's scheduled to begin at 10:30. County residents are up in arms about bad roads in their area and plan to take their concerns to a meeting of the county commission. This story will probably be a package.

10:05 A.M. Reporter #1 and her photographer go out to get some videotape of the roads in question and possibly to talk to a nearby resident (although plenty of interviews will probably be available at the meeting).

10:10 A.M. The three crews are out. All morning the assignment editor and news director have been answering phone calls, listening to the scanner, and doing all kinds of miscellaneous chores in the newsroom. The news director has also been viewing résumé tapes of reporters who want to work for the station. A prospective reporter comes in for an interview.

10:30 A.M. Reporter #4 calls in on the two-way radio and says the drug burn story has been shot, complete with interview. Now he's headed for the relic story.

11:10 A.M. Both the assignment editor and the news director have been on the phone, but the assignment editor thinks he heard something on the police scanner about a bank robbery. He alerts the news director, who calls the police agencies, but she doesn't get much information except that they are responding to a call. The assignment editor continues to monitor the scanners.

11:15 A.M. The assignment editor finally hears the bank robbery address on the police scanner. All the crews are busy, but the station must cover the robbery. Reporter #3 is tied up on the controversial story on zoning and can't be pulled off of it. Reporter #1 is covering the big county roads protest, another important story, and reporter #4 is at the house of the woman who's found the relic. Of all the stories being covered, the last is the one that has to be considered expendable. It's something that can run any day and perhaps can be postponed. The assignment editor therefore pages reporter #4 and asks him to call the station.

11:20 A.M. Reporter #4 calls in after getting his page. The assignment editor tells him to drop the relic story and immediately head to the address of the bank robbery. The assignment editor then gets on the phone with the woman who has the relic and makes his apologies, being careful to explain the situation. He attempts to schedule another time to shoot the story, hoping she won't get angry and call the competition.

11:25 A.M. While all this is going on, the news director has picked up a fire call on the scanner. She contacts the fire department and gets the location, a downtown office building. She immediately checks with the assignment editor to see where the crews are.

11:30 A.M. It's decided that reporter #3 will be pulled off of the zoning story to cover the fire. She's been at the city council meeting for two and a half hours now and should have plenty for at least a VO-bite. She's paged immediately.

11:35 A.M. Reporter #4 arrives on the scene of the bank robbery, gets video, and hopes for an interview with a detective if one is available. It's frequently difficult to get an interview at such times. Police are busy and don't want to release any information prematurely, and bank officials are especially tight-lipped.

11:40 A.M. Reporter #3 calls in. She would have called earlier but was in the midst of an interview. She has plenty for a package, if needed. She is told about the fire and leaves immediately for that location.

11:55 A.M. Both the assignment editor and the news director can tell from the police scanner calls that this is a big fire. The station has a live unit, but it's been out for repairs, and the engineering department says it won't be ready to use until late in the afternoon. The news director, who used to anchor, decides to go on the air with a short interruption in programming to tell about the fire and to say that the station will have a full report that night at six. She avoids saying "live report" because at this point she's not sure the live unit will be ready in time to do a live shot for the 6 P.M. news.

12:05 P.M. Reporter #3 arrives at the fire scene. She radios the station that this is indeed a major fire and asks if the live unit is working. She's told that it's not but it may be later. She's instructed to plan on doing a package, possibly inside her live shot (if one materializes) at the fire scene at 6 P.M. The zoning story will have to be done as a VO-bite because it normally doesn't look good for a reporter to do more than one package per newscast. Packages are the major stories; if a reporter does two, it appears to viewers that the news department doesn't have enough people to cover everything properly (some news departments can't follow this policy because of their small staffs).

12:10 P.M. Reporter #4 is through with the bank robbery and is told to eat lunch quickly and get to his 1:30 assignment on the latest men's fashions. This will be the final, or *kicker*, story in the 6 P.M. newscast. It will be a package. The news director and assignment editor both send out for hamburgers, since too much is going on for them to leave the newsroom.

1:00 P.M. The fire is still going strong, but the crew has gotten some good videotape to use in that night's package. The news director checks again with Engineering to see how the live van repairs are progressing. She's told that with a little luck the unit will be ready by 5 P.M.

1:10 P.M. Reporter #1 returns to the station from her story on the bad roads. It will be a package. She also has to write and edit the VO-bite on the new school story she covered earlier. Because reporter #1 comes in at 5 A.M. every day, the news director tries to get her out of the station by 2 P.M. so her day isn't too long.

1:30 P.M. Reporter #4 has arrived on the fashion story. He shoots it as quickly as possible because he has three stories to write and edit: the marijuana burn (VO-bite), the bank robbery (VO-bite), and the fashion story (package).

1:35 P.M. The night reporter (#6) comes in a little earlier than usual to get to a 2 P.M. story assignment at the local college. It deals with a new computer class for high-school seniors to help them learn more about the advantages of computers as they prepare for college. This should be a package.

2:00 P.M. The producer, both news anchors, the sportscaster, and the weathercaster arrive for work.

Throughout the afternoon the sportscaster will work (generally by himself) to assemble the night's sportscast. This work may include going out with a photographer to shoot a sports story. If this is one of the days the weekend sportscaster works, however, he may cover the story. The average sportscast is allowed three to three and a half minutes, so it can normally be put together easily by one person—although there are those hectic days when the sportscaster needs some help with editing or other tasks.

The weathercaster almost always works alone in assembling the information for the weathercast. This generally includes calling various *weatherwatchers* throughout the area; reporting their observations gives a down-home touch to the weather report (the weatherperson will say something like, "Our weatherwatcher in Lawrenceville, John Williams, says it's been mighty cold there today, with a high of only 29 degrees"). A large part of the weathercaster's work involves assembling the many graphic effects and pictures used to report the weather. He may receive some help with this chore from a production person.

Basically, the same process is repeated for the late news by both the weathercaster and sportscaster. The sportscaster reports late scores and may possibly have a new local sports story; the weathercaster reports new temperatures, perhaps some special weather information, and an updated forecast.

2:05 P.M. The producer checks the wires for any important local or regional news to include in that night's newscast. But so much news has happened already, few if any wire-copy stories will be needed.

2:10 P.M. Reporter #3 radios in that she's now got all she needs for her package on the fire. She asks again about the live van and is told it may be ready by 5 P.M. The assignment editor suddenly remembers that the blood drive—the story that came in the mail that morning—starts at 2:30. With all the commotion over the bank robbery and the fire, he had forgotten about it. The assignment editor asks reporter #3 to go and get a quick VO-bite on the story. One of the anchors will write it.

2:30 P.M. The news director, assignment editor, producer, and both news anchors attend an editorial meeting. The news director and assignment editor brief the producer and anchors on the day's news and get their input on story order and format (e.g., package, VO-bite, VO). Their meeting also provides an opportunity to discuss future story ideas, problem areas that need attention, and other concerns.

3:00 P.M. The editorial meeting is over, and the anchors go about writing scripts and gathering tapes for a series of news teases they will do throughout the afternoon. This, plus helping put the newscast together, will keep them busy. One anchor will write the drug burn script when the videotape comes in. Both will probably rewrite a number of stories the reporters have already finished. Many stations insist that the anchors do this, as it gives a continuity of writing style to the newscast.

The producer has put together the preliminary story rundown for the six o'clock news. Here's what it looks like:

1. *Major fire.* Live shot if possible, with package on the blaze and its damage.
2. *Bank robbery.* VO-bite. Brief interview with detective, shots of the bank.
3. *Marijuana burn.* VO-bite. Shots of marijuana before and during burn. Interview with chief of narcotics.

(*Note:* Stories 1, 2, and 3 are all hard news and need to be run in the order shown, the fire being the most important.)

4. *County roads.* Package, because of controversy.
5. *Zoning controversy.* VO-bite. (This story will run after the county roads story because it's similar.)

(*Note*: Stories 4 and 5 involve citizen protests and might have led the news if the fire hadn't occurred.)

Commercial break #1

6. *Blood drive.* VO-bite. (Written by one of the anchors and edited by photographers, who also help edit the VO-bites and have other duties in the newsroom.)
7. *Computer school.* Package. (This story turned out to be good visually, with a lot of interested students pecking away at the computers.)
8. *New school.* VO-bite. (Ends the first two sections of news on an optimistic note.)

(*Note*: Stories 7 and 8 are both school-related and pair well together.)

Commercial break #2

WEATHER

Commercial break #3

SPORTS

Commercial break #4

9. *Fashions.* Package. (Ends the newscast on a light note.)

END OF NEWSCAST

The producer is a little concerned about the small *story count* (number of stories) in the newscast; however, it's essential that she allow enough time for the live shot on the fire at the beginning of the newscast. This is obviously the big story of the day, and she wants to make sure it's covered adequately. She won't plan definitely on a live shot until she finds out the status of the live unit. If a live shot is used at 6 P.M., more time will be needed for the story.

Here's the quandary she faces from a timing standpoint: If there is a live shot, the anchors will have to begin by saying something about what happened and then introduce the reporter on the scene. The reporter will in turn introduce her own package. At the end she'll probably have an interview with a fire chief or an eyewitness. All of this could easily take up three to four minutes. But if only a package is run, it may take up less than two minutes, including the anchor introduction.

3:10 P.M.   Reporter #6 is back from the computer school story and begins putting his package together.

3:15 P.M.   Reporters #3 and #4 are both back and working on their stories. The news director checks on the live van again and is told that five o'clock is the earliest it can be ready.

4:10 P.M.   The producer hears a police call on the scanner about a wreck on the outskirts of town. The assignment editor has reporter #6 and a photographer rush to the scene because it sounds serious from the talk on the scanner. Reporter #6 has been working on his computer-class package and is almost through. He can finish it in short order when he gets back.

4:40 P.M.   Reporter #6 arrives on the scene of the wreck and radios back to the newsroom that one person has been killed and three seriously injured. He's trying to get an interview and hopes to be back in the station by about 5:20. The producer knows she'll have to make a place for the wreck story because it involves a fatality. She decides to run it as the second story after the one on the fire.

Figure 6.2 shows the revised newscast rundown, with estimated times for the stories, commercial breaks, and weather and sports segments. It also includes a 20-second open, a 15-second close, and four 10-second news teases. These are written by the anchors to promote what's coming up in the next segment and usually include some video on the story. This rundown is not from a computerized newsroom (as is the rundown in Figure 3.1), but it shows the information in much the same way. The calculating is done manually in Figure 6.2.

During the newscast, the producer must be acutely aware of how long each story actually runs as compared with its estimated time shown on the newscast rundown. For example, let's say the fire story runs three and a half minutes instead of three, as originally planned. This means the show is running 30 seconds over. The producer might decide to cut 15 seconds from weather and 15 seconds from sports to gain the 30 seconds she needs. Another option would be to kill either the story on the blood drive or the one on the new school. As both run for 45 seconds, this would make up the 30 seconds needed and give the producer fifteen extra seconds to play with.

If she chooses the latter option, which story should be killed? It depends on the nature and relative importance of the stories. If the blood-drive story

STORY		STORY TIME	RUNNING TIME
	(Newscast Begins)		6:00:00
0.	News Open	:20	6:00:20
1.	Fire, LIVE SHOT & Package	3:00	6:03:20
2.	Fatal wreck VO-bite	:45	6:04:05
3.	Bank Robbery VO-bite	:45	6:04:50
4.	Drug Burn VO-bite	:45	6:05:35
5.	County Roads Package	1:45	6:07:20
6.	Zoning VO-bite	1:00	6:08:20
7.	News tease (computers)	:10	6:08:30
	COMMERCIAL BREAK # 1	2:00	6:10:30
8.	Blood Drive VO-bite	:45	6:11:15
9.	Computers Package	1:45	6:13:00
10.	New School VO-bite	:45	6:13:45
11.	News tease (weather)	:10	6:13:55
	COMMERCIAL BREAK # 2	2:00	6:15:55
12.	WEATHER	4:00	6:19:55
13.	News tease (sports)	:10	6:20:05
	COMMERCIAL BREAK # 3	2:00	6:22:05
14.	SPORTS	3:30	6:25:35
15.	News tease (fashions)	:10	6:25:45
	COMMERCIAL BREAK # 4	2:00	6:27:45
16.	Fashions Package	1:45	6:29:30
17.	Anchors say goodbye	:15	6:29:45
18	Formal close on tape	:15	6:30:00

*** END OF NEWSCAST ***

FIGURE 6.2. This rundown gives the producer a good idea of the time the newscast will take—whether it is too short or *overwritten* (contains too much news). In this case, the show is *tight* (has plenty of news), and there isn't any extra time.

This rundown is similar to the one in Figure 3.1, but it doesn't have as much information. Remember, the rundown in Figure 3.1 came from a computer, whereas this one was done by hand, including the computation of times. It's typical of the rundowns most producers use. The times listed for weather and sports allow for banter between the anchors, the sportscaster, and the weatherperson.

concerns an emergency shortage, the producer will have to kill the story on the new school. But if the blood drive is just an upcoming event and there is no emergency, the school story should be run. The school story is a "today" story, and a lot of children and parents may be watching for it.

4:50 P.M. The producer checks with Engineering again and learns that the live van is finally ready. She knows that the rundown is now as accurate as she can get it. In allocating three minutes for the live shot, she gambled on the live van being ready.

5:05 P.M. The live van is on the way to the live shot. Reporter #3, who is just finishing her package, will leave shortly in a news car to rendezvous with the live van and its crew.

5:20 P.M. Reporter #6 is back with the wreck footage. He quickly writes the story, which is edited by a photographer. This allows him to go back and finish the computer-school story. Since it will begin a little over 11 minutes into the newscast, it doesn't have to be ready by 6 P.M.

5:25 P.M. The live van arrives at the scene of the live shot. The crew checks with fire officials and police to get the best location they'll allow. The crew calls Engineering at the station to let them know they'll be sending over their microwave signal shortly.

5:35 P.M. It's a little late, but the scripts are ready, as well as most of the tapes. The director of the newscast looks over the scripts to see if there are any questions to ask the producer, especially since a live shot is planned at the *top* (beginning) of the news. In many small markets where the news anchors themselves produce the show, the director times the newscast. That's because there is no producer in the control room while the newscast is underway; the producer/anchors are out on the set! The director will want to see if the show is *overproduced* (too much news) or *underproduced* (not enough news).

5:40 P.M. Reporter #3 arrives at the scene of the live shot, checks in with the crew, and tests her *earpiece*, through which she will hear the station's off-the-air audio. The earpiece is the reporter's lifeline to the anchors; without it, she wouldn't hear their introduction to her story or be able to respond to their questions. She also arranges to do a live interview after the package runs.

5:50 P.M. Everyone takes their places to make final preparations for the newscast. By this time everything should be completed, except perhaps the computer-school story by reporter #6, who was out late on the fatal wreck.

5:53 P.M. The live-shot signal suddenly dies! The crew on the live shot calls the station on the two-way radio to say they're having difficulty with either the microwave transmitter or one of the cables. They're working on the problem but are not sure if they can fix it in time. At this point, the producer takes out an alternate script on the fire, to be used if the live shot is not ready. This standby script, edited earlier by reporter #3, treats the fire story as a package. If the standby package is used, the anchors will ad-lib at its close that a crew is on the scene and the station hopes to have a live report later in the newscast. If the live shot does run later, it will not include the package, which will already have been run. The live shot will consist of an update with the latest information, and possibly a live interview. This might be followed by some questions and answers between the anchors and reporter #3.

5:57 P.M. The live-shot signal reappears. The crew notifies the station that the problem has been fixed for now but will need to be checked by Engineering.

6:00 P.M. The newscast begins. The anchors open the show and move to the first story. Reporter #3 is introduced as being live at the scene of the fire. The reporter takes over and talks for a few moments about what's going on now: the fire is out and the cleanup effort is underway. She then introduces her package by saying, "but earlier this afternoon it was a tense situation." At that point her package begins; it tells about how bad the fire was, the injuries, the amount of damage, and many other details. When the package ends, reporter #3 comes on camera again, this time with a fire official. She talks with him about the extent of the damage, the cause of the fire, whether it's arson, and any other significant points not already covered. After the interview she tosses it back to the anchors, who may ask a question if there's time.

The rest of the show goes smoothly. The other hard news stories follow in logical order. The fatal wreck is next because someone was killed. (Keep in mind that this is a medium-to-smaller market, and a death on the highways is considered news; in big markets a traffic death may not even be mentioned unless there are multiple fatalities.) The bank robbery follows because it happened later than the drug burn—it's fresher news. (If the sheriff was destroying half a million dollars worth of drugs, this story would have been much more significant, and probably would have been the lead story if the fire hadn't happened.) The two protest meetings on roads and zoning come next. They're more serious news than the stories scheduled to run in the next section.

The blood-drive story leads the second section (after the commercial break) because it's somewhat serious in nature. It's followed by the computer story and then the story on the new school. The latter is the most upbeat, so it's a good final story for the second section.

The fashion story is an ideal end to the newscast; stations always strive to finish on an up note if possible.

Earlier in the chapter, Figure 6.1 outlined the stories to be covered during this day as of 9 A.M. But as you know, changes had to be made in story coverage as the day progressed. Take a look at Figure 6.3, which summarizes the stories each reporter actually covered during this day, and compare it with Figure 6.1. You can see why reporters must be constantly ready to adapt to any situation.

ACTUAL STORIES COVERED - MONDAY

TIME	STORY (Slug)	TYPE	CREW
8:45am	New School	VO-bite	Reporter/Photog #1
9:00am	City Council (Zoning)	VO-bite	Reporter/Photog #3
10:00am	Drug Burn	VO-bite	Reporter/Photog #4
10:30am	County Roads	Package	Reporter/Photog #1
11:35am	Bank Robbery	VO-bite	Reporter/Photog #4
12:05	Fire	Package & LIVE	Reporter/Photog #3
1:30pm	Fashions	Package	Reporter/Photog #4
2:00pm	Computer	Package	Reporter/Photog #6
2:30pm	Blood Drive	VO-bite	Reporter/Photog #3
4:40pm	Fatal wreck	VO-bite	Reporter/Photog #6
7:30pm	Chemicals/Lake (for late news)	Package	Reporter/Photog #6

FIGURE 6.3.   This is the final rundown of stories actually covered for the day as of 6 P.M. You'll note that things started out as planned, but the bank robbery and the fire changed some reporters' assignments. Reporter #4 had to drop his relic story and head for the bank robbery. Reporter #3 was pulled off of the city council zoning story to go to the fire. Her zoning story was then turned into a VO-bite, since she was going live and already had a package on the fire. Also, reporter #6 had to rush out to cover the fatal wreck but managed to get back in time to write that story and finish his computer package as well.

This chart shows only news covered until 6 P.M. Something else might very well happen at night, forcing reporter #6 to cover another story, such as a shooting or perhaps a train wreck. If things get too involved, an additional reporter and photographer will be called in to help. This is the way it is in news—there are plenty of scheduled stories to cover, but many unscheduled ones as well.

6:40 P.M.   The news director meets with the producer to discuss the 6 P.M. news and any problems that occurred. The news director makes a note to check with Engineering the next morning about any equipment malfunctions that surfaced during the day, as well as during the newscast. She also makes notes about the reporters' stories. She will talk with each of them the next day about any problems with their stories, or to commend them on a job well done.

The news director and producer then turn their attention to the late news and decide which stories from 6 P.M. will be rewritten and used again. As a matter of course, if a reporter does a package for the six o'clock news, it is recut to a VO-bite for the late news. Sometimes the opposite is done—a VO-bite is used at six and a package is used later. Many news directors go home after the 6 P.M. newscast and let the producer make decisions on the late news.

There's just not enough time to repeat all the six o'clock stories in the late news, so the producer picks the most important. They run, but are re-edited and rewritten first. The producer is concerned about one of the biggest complaints viewers all over the country have about late news: they feel it's a rehash of the six o'clock newscast. But you certainly can't drop the stories on the bank robbery and the drug bust. These stories must be run again because a large number of viewers haven't seen the early newscast. If they don't see some coverage of the big stories, they'll think the station has missed them.

Reporter #3 has had a long day, but she has to come back and recut a package for the late news because the fire was such a big story. She will also recut the zoning VO-bite to another VO-bite because of the story's impact. All the reporters were told earlier in the afternoon what they needed to do for the late news, so there would be no misunderstanding about what was expected from each of them. This way, after the 6 P.M. news the producer has at her disposal a number of rewritten and re-edited stories: reporter #4 recut his piece on the marijuana burn to a 25-second VO. He did the same thing for the bank robbery story. Before the morning reporter (#1) left earlier in the afternoon, she re-edited the story on the new school to a 20-second VO and the one on the county roads to a VO-bite (we'll assume VO-bites will run 45 seconds, as they did on the 6 P.M. news).

Reporter #6 will recut his report on the fatal accident to a 25-second VO, but he also has to leave shortly to cover a new story for the late news on chemicals in the lake. The producer will not use the fashion, blood drive, or computer-school stories for the late news. The blood drive story will not be used again because there was no critical need for blood; the fashion story was meant for a one-time-only showing; the computer-school story could be run again as a VO or VO-bite, but she decides against it because there's more than enough important world and national news to include in tonight's late news.

7:00 P.M. Reporter #6 leaves for his 7:30 assignment. A group of residents is concerned because a plant is dumping chemicals into a creek that feeds a lake near their homes. Earlier, the assignment editor sent the night photographer to the creek to get daytime footage of any visible pollution. This will be included in the reporter's package for the late newscast.

7:10 P.M. The news director finally leaves for the day after putting in about ten and a half hours on the job. Sometimes she'll stay even later in the evening to view audition tapes and sort through the mountain of mail she gets. This is the "quiet time" for her, now that the station staff has left and the phones aren't ringing much. It's frequently impossible for her to accomplish much administrative work during the day because of all the distractions.

7:30 P.M. The producer has been sorting through the world and national news from the wire machine, deciding what will be used tonight. Unlike 6 P.M. newscasts, late newscasts are almost always a mix of the top world, national, and local news of the day. At six o'clock the viewers have either just seen a network newscast, or will at 6:30, so stations don't want to include world or national news in what is traditionally a local newscast. But at 10 or 11 P.M., it's been hours since many viewers were exposed to any news, and they need the complete picture. A number of people don't watch the 6 P.M. news at all, because they're not home from work in time.

7:45 P.M. The producer has her final rundown for the 11 P.M. show and meets with the co-anchors to lay out which scripts each anchor will write. The re-written local stories she uses from the early news may have to be rewritten once more: the anchors may need to put them into language they feel more comfortable with. The producer has also selected videotape reports from the network evening news program or those sent down by satellite earlier in the day. In addition, there will be a late network feed of stories if there is any late-breaking world or national news.

9:15 P.M. Reporter #6 has returned from the meeting with the people concerned about chemicals in the lake. This story will be a package for 11, as planned.

10:30 P.M. Scripts and edited tapes are ready for the director by this time.

11:00 P.M. The late news finally begins on what has been a very active day for this newsroom.

11:30 P.M. The late news is over. The producer writes a memo to the news director concerning anything that went wrong during the 11 P.M. newscast, including equipment problems that might need attention the next morning. One item in the note will be a reminder to have Engineering check out the live van and make sure there's no problem with the equipment. They almost lost the live shot at six (you'll remember that the crew just barely got the signal back up in time for the newscast).

11:45 P.M.   The two news anchors and just about everyone else leave for the night after straightening up the newsroom a bit.

11:50 P.M.   The producer finally leaves after checking the stories planned for the next day to get an idea of what tomorrow's newscast will look like (unless there are new developments).

What you've read in this chapter should give you an idea of an average day in a TV newsroom and how the staff responds to changing events. Obviously, many scenarios could develop, and the news team has to be flexible in order to meet the demands of each day.

III BUSINESS ASPECTS OF TV NEWS

7 TV Markets

You've undoubtedly seen the term *TV market*, or just *market*, in *TV Guide* or some other publication. Market size is very important because it determines the size of a station's newsroom and the amount of money spent on the news effort. Thus, it also affects things of immediate concern to you, such as employment prospects and salary.

A TV market is a geographic area served by a group of TV stations, which are usually located in the main city in that market. Examples of markets are New York, Chicago, Los Angeles, Dallas, Miami, Atlanta, and Cincinnati. In general, a market has at least three TV stations (one for each network) and a public broadcasting station (PBS); the larger markets may have one or more independent stations as well. You'll find some smaller markets with just two TV stations and others with only one.

A TV market's numerical size, or *ranking*, is determined by the number of homes with TV sets located in that market. This count is part of the *ratings* conducted by special national services. A market may not be very big in terms of geographical area, but it may have a dense population and therefore a large number of potential viewers. A complete listing of all markets according to size can be found in the *Broadcasting Yearbook*, an annually published resource of important industry information (Washington, D.C.: Broadcasting Publications, Inc.). However, since ratings are determined at least four times a year everywhere (and all the time in the big markets), market listings are available at other times of the year in a number of broadcasting publications. There are always minor fluctuations, with markets moving up or down a few places, depending on what the latest ratings show.

How Many Markets?

The United States has approximately 210 to 213 TV markets. The number varies from year to year, but it normally falls within that range (later we'll see why the total changes). The smaller the number, the bigger the market or ranking. For example, New York is number one because it's the country's most populous market. Los Angeles is number two, Chicago is three, and so on.

If you were to look at a U.S. map with market lines drawn on it (as well as county lines) but no state lines, there would appear to be about 210 to 213 "states" of varying sizes. Each of these "market states," as we'll call them, would contain a number of counties.

Nielsen and Arbitron are the two national ratings services. When they take their ratings, they find out which TV stations a county primarily watches. A county is included in the TV market that is watched by most of the viewers in that county. For instance, if 42% of the viewers in a county between Memphis and Nashville watches Nashville TV stations, and 38% watches Memphis TV stations, that county is considered part of the Nashville market. This could be the case even if the county is actually located closer to Memphis.

When all the counties in the United States have been assigned to markets, market lines are drawn. Every county in each market has been found to primarily watch TV stations in that market. In many cases, these new "market states" cross actual state lines. That's because a television signal is generally transmitted in all directions. The signal of a station located near a state line may go into a neighboring state, and some of that state's counties may be included in the TV station's market.

The stations determining a market may not even be in the same city. One example is the Mobile, Alabama–Pensacola, Florida market. The CBS and NBC affiliates are in Mobile, but the ABC station is located in Pensacola. The CBS and NBC affiliates cover a number of Alabama counties, but because they're close to the Florida panhandle, they also broadcast into some Florida counties, including the one in which the city of Pensacola is located. Likewise, the ABC affiliate's signals reach not only parts of the Florida panhandle but also the section of Alabama in which Mobile is located. The nature of broadcast signals and population centers creates some oddly structured markets. This presents some stations with the interesting challenge of covering news important to several different cities or states.

Of course, you'll never see TV market maps in a geography book. They're usually found only in advertising agencies, TV stations, and the offices of the ratings services. Advertisers use them to see exactly what area is covered by a particular market's TV stations. This information helps them decide where to spend their advertising dollars.

Occasional variations in the total number of markets are generally the result of the appearances and disappearences of the very smallest markets. For example, if a TV station goes on the air where there was none before, a new market may be created if the station gets enough of a county's viewers. Or if the only station in a market goes off the air, that market may then disappear (obviously, this would be a very small market, barely able to support one TV station).

You may ask why we have the number of markets we do. It's because of the way the country developed and where people settled and built cities. Population centers that contained high concentrations of people were the places where it was financially feasible to build TV stations. The East has a number of large cities and, therefore, many large markets. Out West, where the population is much sparser, the markets tend to be fewer in number but bigger in area. These markets are larger in geographic size because of the generally rural territory that surrounds many of them (see Figure 7.1).

Let's take Albuquerque as an example. In 1988 Albuquerque was ranked 55th in the country in terms of its number of viewers; however, the physical size of its market is due to the rural nature of much of New Mexico. With two exceptions, there isn't another city in that state large enough to support a TV station. The towns in New Mexico are too small for a station to sell enough commercials to make a profit. Consequently, the Albuquerque market is allowed to cover not only most of New Mexico but also parts of southern Colorado, western Texas, and eastern Arizona. Albuquerque TV stations are able to cover this large area with the use of *translators.*

What Are Translators?

In order to serve thinly populated areas with no local TV stations, some stations in distant markets have been allowed to set up what are commonly called translators to give these rural areas some measure of television reception. A translator—an electronic device that consists of a TV receiver and a low-power TV transmitter—does nothing more than receive and retransmit the main station's signal. To prevent interference, a station on channel 13, for example, would be received by the translator on channel 13 and retransmitted to a rural section of the state on another channel in the ultra-high frequency (UHF) range (such as 24, 47, 62).

Because of the density of population in the East, translators are rarely found there. They're primarily used in the western states to provide television reception to people in remote rural areas that would otherwise not be served by TV stations.

Some people purchase satellite reception equipment to give them a greater variety of TV choices. Perhaps you have driven through a sparsely populated region and seen a satellite dish behind a house. This may have been the only way that family could receive television signals.

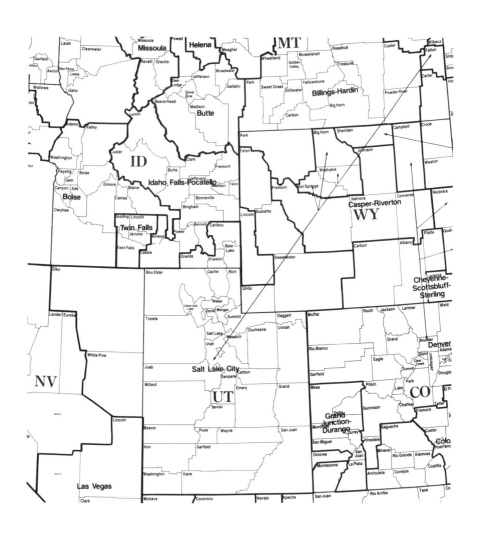

How Does Market Size Affect Your Career?

Market size determines, to some extent, the amount of money a station spends on its various departments, including news. Why? Sponsors pay for TV commercials according to the size of the audience that will see them. In larger markets, more money is paid for the same commercials because of the greater number of viewers they reach. Stations in larger markets thus make more money and are able to be more generous with their news departments in terms of salaries, staff size, and equipment.

Thus, a station's size, the strength and resources of its news department, and the salaries and opportunities it can offer are usually a direct reflection of the market size. There are, of course, occasional exceptions, sometimes warranted and sometimes not. For example, a well-known anchor in a mid-sized market may receive a salary considered too large for that market. This may be simply because the anchor gets very high ratings and is valuable to the station. It's just good business sense to pay him well enough to keep him around. On the other hand, sometimes you'll find a station that is notorious for paying salaries well below the average in its market. Sometimes resources are allocated inappropriately. It's rare that you'll find a station too well equipped, but you will find some with inadequate technical facilities for the quality demanded by

---

FIGURE 7.1.   Two television markets in the United States: New York City, which has the greatest population, and Salt Lake City, which is physically the largest. Both maps were drawn on the same scale; note how much larger Salt Lake City is. However, in market rankings, New York is number one while Salt Lake City usually falls in the 39 to 41 range.

Because of its geographic location, the New York market also covers a small part of New York State and includes sections of New Jersey, Connecticut, and even a county in Pennsylvania. The Salt Lake City market not only encompasses the entire state of Utah, but reaches into Nevada, Idaho, Wyoming, and counties in Montana and Colorado. Because Utah is a rural area and has no other market, Salt Lake City stations have been allowed to set up translators, which strengthen signals and retransmit them to specific rural areas. Translators are the only means of getting TV signals to rural areas. Individuals who own satellite dishes, of course, have other options. Counties in Wyoming and Montana that are separated from the main market receive Salt Lake City station signals through cable television.

If there were a city in the southern part of Utah with a large enough population to support TV stations with advertising revenue, then stations probably would have been built there. In that case, Utah would have two TV markets today instead of one, and our hypothetical market would be the supplier of TV signals to the southern part of the state. (Maps copyright © 1989, The Arbitron Company. All rights reserved.)

their markets. Obviously, the quality of the news broadcasts at such stations is low.

We can look at it this way: the bigger the market, the bigger the news departments of the TV stations in that market. Salaries are higher in these markets, and the overall news effort is much stronger. Conversely, the smaller the market, the lower the news salaries and the smaller the staff. Nevertheless, in the highly competitive TV industry, there are more job opportunities, especially for newcomers, in markets and stations with weaker news efforts and lower salaries. So despite their drawbacks, the smaller markets may offer important opportunities for you to enter the industry.

8 The Ratings Game

TV ratings are the only tangible evidence of any show's success or failure. Many people are skeptical about ratings, saying that "good" shows get the axe when they shouldn't. Although ratings are not the only factor in determining a show's success or failure, they are, for better or worse, an important measure relied upon by broadcasting decision makers. Naturally, when a new program goes on the air, everyone hopes it will do well. A great deal of expense has gone into putting the concept together, and a number of episodes have already been ordered. Usually, when a show flops, a lot of money goes down the drain.

Points and Shares

When you hear the word *ratings*, it's often accompanied by the terms *ratings points* and *share*. These are statistical units of measurement, and their study can be quite complex. Simply put, ratings points estimate in percentages the total number of people watching a show at a given time. For example, if a show has a rating of 20, this means that 20 percent of all the *TV households* (homes owning at least one TV set) in a particular market are watching the show. If the area being tested is a single market with 100,000 TV households, 20 percent means 20,000 viewing households. If the area being tested is the entire nation, a 20 rating means that 20% of all the nation's TV households are watching the show!

A decrease of one ratings point represents a sizeable drop in viewers, especially in the case of a nationally televised program. This means advertisers would either not buy commercials in the program or, at the very least, pay less for them. However, if a program's ratings increase by several points, the network or station is delighted because this indicates that more viewers are watching. The next time a company buys commercials in that show it will probably have to pay more because the show now has more viewers.

The share is the percentage of viewers watching a show in relation to the percentage watching competing programs. Unlike ratings points, which reflect a percentage of the total households owning TVs, shares are a percentage of the number of households watching TV during a specific time period. For example, Program A may have a 15 share, Program B a 35 share, Program C a 40 share, and all others a 10 share. This means that of all the shows broadcast during a given time period (100 percent), program C is the top show, with a 40 percent viewership; Program B is second with 35 percent, and so on. A show with a very high share may still have low total viewership—for instance, a program that runs in the early morning hours or late at night. Remember, share has nothing to do with the number of people watching; it only refers to one program's standing in relation to others that run at the same time. Because advertisers want to know how many total viewers a program has, they're much more concerned with ratings points than shares.

Second Seasons

In the 1950s and early 1960s, a network show going on the air in the fall was almost guaranteed to run the entire year. The people behind the program may have realized that at some point it would not return, but at least it was assured a one-year run.

As the years went by, ratings were taken more often to help network executives decide if a show would continue on the air for a full year or be cut short in midseason. The term *second season* was coined to describe a replace-ment show put on the air, usually by January, to fill the time slot of a show cancelled because of poor ratings. Advertisers did not want to continue buying commercials on low-rated shows—certainly not at the prime rates many of them were paying—so network executives had to make a change.

Many second-season shows had not been selected to air the previous fall but had been considered first runners-up. Sometimes these replacement shows did well enough to be renewed the following fall.

Big-Market Ratings

Today, ratings are taken virtually all the time in the big markets. These big-market ratings help the networks decide whether a network show stays on the air. The top markets involve a huge cross-section of people, and it's thought that if a program does poorly in these markets, it will never get a large enough audience countrywide to ensure its success. Because of this continuous ratings process, some shows have a very short life.

In areas outside the big markets, ratings are taken only in February, May, July, and November. Consequently, changes in local programming don't occur as often as those on the network level.

Smaller-Market Ratings

So far we've been talking about network programs and the concerns of network executives on the national level. What about local stations? Are their concerns the same? In a word, yes. Local stations have the same hopes, not only for their network's programs but also for shows they air themselves when the network is not supplying a program—usually during some midmorning hours, late in the afternoon, and early in the evening. During these time periods, local stations often buy and air *syndicated shows*.

Syndicated shows are non-network shows sold to individual TV stations. These can be original programming (such as some talk and game shows and a few prime-time quality shows) or simply packages of old movies and reruns. Stations can make a lot of money with these programs if the ratings are good, because the station can keep the revenues from all the available commercial time. During network programs, local affiliates (stations) share commercial time with the network. The local station thus gets the higher-quality programming at no cost, but its revenues from such shows are lower than they'd be if the station ran its own shows.

Most local stations will put a show that they buy or produce on the air for at least half a year or longer. The fact is, stations usually pay so much money for the right to broadcast the average syndicated show that they must run it as long as possible in the hope it will catch on. Many stations have had to take a show off after several months because of low ratings, but because they had purchased the rights to run it for two to three years, they were forced to continue paying for it. It's like buying a new car and financing it without getting insurance. After just a few months you have a collision, and the car is totally destroyed. But because you didn't have insurance, you must continue paying for a car you can't use anymore. This should give you an idea of how a station's general manager feels when a syndicated show fails badly in the ratings. He can't use it anymore, but he still has to pay for it.

A general manager may try to bring back a failing show the next year in a different time slot, hoping the change will improve its ratings. This may work, depending on what the competition is, or it may fail worse than the first time. In some ways it's like rolling dice in Las Vegas.

You may say, Why doesn't a station buy one of those really popular shows that did well on the network before it was available to local stations in syndication? That's a pretty good idea, and many general managers do this; however, they then face another type of problem. They have to pay such high prices for these shows, the big question is not "Will the show do well in the ratings?" but "Will it do well enough to justify the high price I'm going to have to ask for commercials, just to make a little profit?"

Until the mid-eighties, many shows were bought by local stations for two to three years. The station was given the right to run the program a certain number of times (if they wanted to) within that period. Now, however, some shows are sold for just one year. This is mainly due to the high cost of many programs and the reluctance of general managers to tie themselves down to three-year contracts for shows that may not do well. With a one-year contract, if a program fares poorly, the station's losses won't be as high. There are still a few three-year contracts, however.

TV Ratings and TV News

A highly rated newscast can be a big plus to a station in many different ways. Thus, every effort should be made to have the best news show possible. Obviously, if the ratings are good, commercials sold during the newscast will be worth more, which means increased revenues for the station. As many as 20 to 22 thirty-second commercials could run in a typical half-hour news program; that's a lot of commercial dollars. There are other, less tangible benefits to having a strong newscast. Certainly, the morale of the station is bolstered.

In addition, many professionals in the business will tell you that a first-rate TV news department can attract viewers to some of the station's other shows. Ideally, of course, a station makes a strong effort in all its programming, and every show reinforces the others and the station as a whole. In reality, a station usually has to use its strengths to compensate for its weaknesses. A local affiliate can't do much about the network programs it carries, but if they are weak, an effective promotional strategy, a strong news program, and shrewd management can still result in strong programming.

General managers want a good *lead-in* (the show before) and *lead-out* (the show after) to their local newscasts. The lead-in is usually a syndicated or locally produced show; the lead-out is often, but not always, the network news. In some time zones (Central and Mountain), this is reversed. The network news leads into the local newscast; the lead-out is a syndicated show. If these shows are successful, they should enhance the success of the station's newscast to some degree. But unlike network shows, a news program can't be cancelled.

The news must run, and generally in a specific time period. What happens when a newscast does poorly in the ratings, even though it is framed by fairly good lead-in and lead-out shows? Since it can't be replaced, what can be done? Well, there's no simple answer to that question; it depends on a number of things.

The first big factor is, How much of a commitment to news does the losing station have, and will the ownership agree to spend the money needed to bring about substantial change? A general manager who knows he can't get financial support from the station owner yet is honest about the situation with his news director should be congratulated. At least both of these people can try to fashion the best news product possible, even though there's not much money to work with.

The second factor is an offshoot of the first: How much money can the station spend to revamp its news product and make it more appealing to the viewers? Will it be enough to do the job? If the money isn't there, then less expensive measures can be tried, such as painting the news set, changing the music, or using new camera angles. In any case, the general manager and the news director must look realistically at their budget and decide if the money they have to spend is enough to make a difference.

The third factor is, How big or significant is the competition? It's possible that a certain network may do so well in a town that its local affiliate may simply be too strong to overcome. That station's local news is probably the ratings leader and will be very difficult to dislodge. A crafty general manager might push to get his newscast into second place if he thinks he has enough resources to do so. His station would make more money in second place and be ready to make a move for first if the leading station ever ran into major problems like losing its top anchors.

Most broadcasting professionals realize that if their newscast is getting poor ratings, something is definitely wrong—and probably a number of things. Knowing this, they take action to identify and correct the problems. This generally means calling in a consultant who can help the station formulate a new strategy for the newscast. The consultant will gather as much information as possible on the market, the competing stations (especially their on-air personalities), and the client station. The consultant wants to know the strengths and weaknesses of all the stations in the market and how their air personalities are perceived by viewers. When a station's ratings are poor, it almost always takes a comprehensive plan to improve them substantially.

Of course, some smaller station owners would like to pull ahead but just don't have the money. But many larger companies that do have the funds decide not to make any changes or improvements. Some of them approach the situation from a "cart before the horse" viewpoint. They say to their news directors, "When your ratings come up, we'll get you that equipment you want and the additional reporters." The truth is, you'll rarely find a station that has significantly brought up its ratings without some expense and a lot of work.

Some TV stations have very astute management when it comes to keeping expenses down and turning a profit, but their news departments are usually sadly lacking. The station owners do not appear to be interested in having a number-one news operation (which could, down the road, bring in new business); their approach is strictly from a short-term dollars-and-cents standpoint. If they feel it will cost too much to bring up the ratings, or take too long to recoup their investment, they won't spend the money.

News departments at stations with this perspective are invariably smaller than those at competing stations, and the salaries they pay are usually far lower. Employment at such a station may not be your long-term career goal, but it may represent a decent early career opportunity, simply because the competition for jobs won't be as tough.

Demographics

You may be familiar with the term *demographics*. As far as TV ratings are concerned, it's the breakdown by sex and age group of who is looking at various shows. In the early days of television there was less concern about specific age groups or gender. But as the years passed and the ratings-takers became more sophisticated in data collection, demographics became more important.

As you know, there are some products—pantyhose and perfume, for example—that are primarily of interest to women. Shaving cream and sports magazines are primarily of interest to men. In addition to women and men, other demographic groups, such as teens, young marrieds, and senior citizens, each have their own interests. If you're a manufacturer of a product designed for young marrieds with children, you want to buy commercials in shows that have large numbers of viewers in that group. You certainly don't want your commercial to run in a show watched only by teens or senior citizens.

This is known as *targeting* your audience. It's not new—advertisers have been doing it for some time. Even if a newscast, or any show, does well in the ratings, its demographics are considered seriously by today's advertisers. It's something every general manager has to think about when planning local programming.

Let's say you're an auto-parts manufacturer. Auto parts have been shown to be generally of greater interest to men than to women, so you might place commercials on ESPN, the cable sports network, which is heavily watched by male viewers. Or you could put commercials on one of the car-racing shows on TNN (The Nashville Network). The Big Three networks offer many opportunities for targeting, but cable TV, which reaches increasing numbers of viewers, has broken the spectrum into much more specific demographic groups. This has enabled advertisers to make their targeting even more precise.

9 Consultants

Why Use Consultants?

If a station has hired a good news director and good personnel, why should it need a consultant? One of the primary reasons is research. The big consulting firms use sophisticated methods to find out what viewers in a market really like or dislike about stations and their on-air talent. The big firms have people with special training in market research. Even large TV stations cannot afford to do such research on their own.

A consultant also offers an objective viewpoint. Some problems, solutions, and opportunities are more apparent to someone who is not an employee of the station. Good consultants also bring to any station a tremendous wealth of experience in pinpointing and solving the problems of TV stations. Much of this comes from having consulted for a great number and variety of stations. A highly experienced TV station employee may have worked in half a dozen stations; a seasoned consultant will have performed detailed work for many, many more. In addition, most consultants come from broadcasting backgrounds; many are former TV news directors or executive producers or have held similar positions.

It's important to note that these consultants work only with television stations. All their time and energies are aimed at coming up with suggestions to help their client stations improve ratings and make more money. You won't find a TV consultant working one month at a TV station and then two months later assisting another company in devising a marketing plan for its product. Television consulting has become so sophisticated that it requires a full-time effort.

Consultants advise on virtually every aspect of the news department operation—the writing, the editing, the way the newscast is produced, the news set, colors, the anchors' delivery—you name it. In many cases a consultant's main job is to fine-tune what is already considered a good newscast.

But sometimes consultants are called on to orchestrate a massive rebuilding. This is frequently done in third-place stations, which obviously need more help than the others. The consultants come in, do their research, and make their recommendations. As management makes the suggested changes, the consultants continue to advise the station on the effects those changes are having and what additional steps may need to be taken.

Consultants sometimes devise very innovative but drastic measures to boost a station's audience. Even if such changes are ultimately successful, they may initially prompt a negative reaction simply because they represent change. For example, there were numerous complaints about the "happy talk" format that evolved in the early 1970s, largely as a result of input from consultants. Prior to that time, newscasts at most stations were delivered in a rather formal, straightforward manner. Commercials generally separated the weather and sports segments, as well as the people who filled those jobs. It was almost as though they were all in different rooms; there was no interaction among the anchors.

One notable consultant saw this as something that desperately needed changing. He was astute enough to realize that viewers wanted "friends" in their home at night. This is why the Huntley/Brinkley team and Walter Cronkite became so popular—they were "nice people" with whom the viewers were comfortable. The consultant knew viewers would respond to the same warm qualities in their local anchors as well. He also knew the anchors should be perceived as liking one another. Surveys have shown that viewers are uncomfortable when they sense that the anchors aren't compatible, that the "chemistry" is wrong. If this happens, they may change the channel.

Thus was born the "happy talk" format. It's really very simple: as the anchors read the news, they interact from time to time. When they turn to the weatherperson, you'll hear some warm words and possibly a little laughter over something amusing. After the weather, perhaps more talk is exchanged among the anchors and weatherperson. The same sort of casual conversation is made at the beginning and end of the sportscast.

It took a little time to get accustomed to, but with some modifications, the format worked—and it helped turn a number of losing stations into winners. Today, virtually every newscast has the now-refined "happy talk" format.

In some cases, consultants advise stations to make changes that superficially seem unwarranted but may actually be effective and appropriate. The print media and portions of the public may not immediately appreciate the move and be highly critical. This is especially true when an anchor change is made. If the fired anchor has been around for a while and didn't seem to have an obvious problem, the entertainment reporter for a newspaper may come up with "good copy" by taking the station to task for the firing. The print reporter, however, does not have access to important survey data from the consultant, which may have revealed a problem with the anchor that could not be corrected (for example, the anchor may have been too young or too old). The fired anchor may have tended to "turn off" the very group of viewers the news department is now trying to attract (the competition across town may be making inroads with a new, younger anchor). Naturally, the station will have had to fire the anchor without making this information public.

The age issue can be especially touchy. Now more than ever before, business in general has become sensitive to this issue; age discrimination lawsuits are more common today. However, harsh reality may dictate that a station let an anchor go because of age. Extensive research may reveal that the anchor no longer effectively appeals to the audience. Usually, though, more than just the question of age is involved in releasing an anchor who has been in a market for a long time. The consultant may have discovered that the research surveys revealed another problem that was even more serious.

You know the saying, "If it ain't broke, don't fix it." Most news directors live by that motto. If their newscast is doing well in the ratings and not showing any signs of slipping, they wouldn't think of making a change. If someone is fired, you can be sure it was done for a definite reason and was not rushed into.

Consultants first gained prominence in the 1970s, when news directors in a number of markets were puzzling over the same problem. They knew that both their own news product and their competition's were good, but how could their newscast be improved to make it stand out over the competition? What could they do to make it special? A consultant was called in to come up with an approach to this problem. Today, the majority of TV stations probably use consultants to maintain or improve their market standing.

The Consultant in Action

Generally, the first thing a consultant does is take a survey of the market to find out each station's strong and weak points. For example, let's say we have three TV stations in a particular market: AAA-TV, BBB-TV, and CCC-TV. A consultant working for AAA-TV has her staff conduct a detailed telephone survey of a certain number of viewers in the area. The survey is designed to be fair to all the stations in the market, because only in this way can the consultant get accurate information about each one's strengths and weaknesses. Part of the survey deals with personalities—who's liked, who's not, and the reasons why. Armed with these facts, the consultant can make recommendations to the client station about steps to take to improve its ratings.

Let's assume that AAA-TV is in third place and has been for a very long time. BBB-TV is in second place, and the leader is CCC-TV; these stations have also been in their respective standings for years. In looking over the results of the survey, the consultant finds that CCC-TV is a favorite of many viewers because of a long-time but aging anchorman. The newscast is not bad, although it's not as far ahead of the others in quality as the ratings might indicate. The consultant also discovers that viewers don't really have a strong conviction about CCC-TV; they watch mainly out of habit.

The survey shows that BBB-TV has a decent anchor team but no standouts. Its newscasts, like those of CCC-TV, are adequate but not award-winners. Even though both BBB-TV and CCC-TV have the usual weekend public affairs shows, neither are heavily involved in the community.

What has the consultant learned that's useful to her client station, AAA-TV? First of all, the survey revealed a weakness at the leading station, CCC-TV: the anchor there is popular but not exceptional. Because viewers watch the station out of habit more than for any other reason, they're considered "*soft.*" This means they can be attracted to another station with a better newscast or anchors. The consultant has also found that CCC-TV's newscast is really not outstanding and can probably be beaten by a more visually attractive and better-produced newscast.

How about BBB-TV? Are there any weaknesses there? Yes, but mainly because the station's newscast is considered average and doesn't seem to make an impression one way or the other. There are no strong viewer reactions to BBB-TV or its anchors. This is considered a good sign by the consultant: there isn't another well-entrenched personality to overcome (like the anchor at CCC-TV), making it easier to establish a new anchor at AAA-TV.

Another possible advantage for AAA-TV is that neither of its competitor stations or their anchors have any kind of active community involvement. The consultant knows that a big drive to have AAA-TV's anchors make public service promotional announcements and appear before civic groups will set AAA-TV apart as the one station that is really concerned about the community.

All the survey findings about the competitors are certainly useful, but what does the survey say about AAA-TV? The station has gone through a number of news anchors over the years, primarily because of low pay. The survey finds that overall, these anchors have lacked credibility and really haven't appeared to work as a team on the set. The station's young sportscaster, who is attractive and really knows his sports, scores well on personality and on-set demeanor, despite poor ratings for the show as a whole. The weatherperson, however, is shown by the survey to be a real problem. He's been a fixture for years but has a personality that just doesn't appeal to many viewers. As a matter of fact, some people volunteered comments to the consultant's survey takers regarding their dislike for the weatherperson.

This is a red flag for the consultant! People normally hesitate to say something negative about a person, especially to a stranger on the phone. But when they volunteer this type of comment about a TV personality, it's considered a serious indication that the individual may be hurting the newscast and driving away viewers. In a 400-phone-call survey, as few as 10 voluntary negative responses may mean someone has to be fired for the good of the newscast. It's brutal, but remember—TV is a business, and if someone isn't buying your product, you'd better change it to make it more appealing.

The survey also shows that the male anchor is perceived to be too youthful, lacking the maturity needed to compete with the other anchors in the market. In contrast, the survey reveals that the female anchor, who has been on the job only nine months, projects a positive image on the news set and delivers the news with credibility.

Revamping the Newscast

The consultant meets with the general manager of AAA-TV and presents all the information she has gathered. It's obvious to the consultant, and the general manager, that big steps will have to be taken to change the image of AAA-TV's news product.

The station will immediately (although confidentially) begin to look for a new male anchor. The new anchor will have to be older and more credible than the present one in order to compete with the more mature, established anchor at the leading station, CCC-TV. A search will also be launched for a new weatherperson because of the high negative response to the current weatherman in the consultant's surveys. The female anchor and the sportscaster will be asked to stay. As for the news director, if she is receptive and bright enough to deal with the coming changes, she will probably be asked to stay on the job too. Terminations won't happen immediately; replacements must be found first.

The consultant tells the general manager of AAA-TV that to get and keep talented anchors, he must upgrade their salaries. This includes recognizing the present female anchor with a decent pay increase.

With the news and weather anchor searches underway, the consultant spends time in the newsroom with the news director to identify problem areas. Is there enough equipment? Does it get proper servicing? Are there sufficient reporters and photographers to do the job? Another area of concern is writing.

Stories that are poorly written and edited can leave viewers with more questions than answers. This may cause them to change the channel.

Other big changes are in the works too. Remember, AAA-TV has been in the back seat for a long time. Once everything is in place and promotion begins, AAA-TV must look like a totally revamped station. That's why a new set with a new color scheme is being built under the watchful eye of the station artist. New colors are even planned for the news cars. In addition, new music will be used for the open and close of the news. The opening music must help create a different and exciting feeling about the upcoming newscast. Combined with a well-done visual open, it will give viewers the impression they're going to see something worth watching.

Let's say the replacement news and weather anchors are hired and have arrived for work. The new set has been completed and the audio and video for the new open and close are ready. Does the station blow its horn now? Not yet! As anxious as the staff is, promotion must be delayed. Everyone has to work together for a while—maybe several weeks or more—until all the rough edges are smoothed out. The new staff members will have a chance to get acquainted during this period, which will help them interact more effectively on the air.

When the time is right, a comprehensive plan of promotion will be launched to include newspapers, radio, perhaps billboards, and certainly plenty of personality profiles run periodically during the day on AAA-TV. These are usually 30 seconds to a minute in length and are designed to show a little of the human qualities or experience of the anchors so the viewers will get to know them better. The anchor team will also be sent into the field from time to time to speak at civic-group functions and other gatherings. It's all part of a plan to publicize the fact that a new and more professional team is in town—one that should be checked out!

You may be wondering why all this is necessary. Well, for one thing, viewers tend to be set in their ways and resistant to change. Something unfamiliar must be extensively and creatively publicized to arouse their interest. If viewers are impressed by your publicity and decide to tune in to AAA-TV's newscast, it had better be worth it. If the new look and presentation are not obvious, they will probably go back to their old station. Should that happen, it will be harder than ever to get those viewers to watch your newscast again. They chose not to watch AAA-TV for some reason in the past, and unless it looks a lot different to them after the big promotion, they'll think nothing has really changed.

The new male anchor should be a prime attraction, and it is hoped that he will outshine the more established anchor at CCC-TV. In place of the former AAA-TV weatherperson who was driving viewers away is another weathercaster who, it is hoped, will attract a larger audience. Even with all the changes, it may take awhile for the ratings to turn around.

In the example used here, the leading station (CCC-TV) has only average involvement in the community. But if it were very active in community affairs, with lots of popular anchors and a good news product, then the job of turning AAA-TV around would be much more difficult. In that case, the consultant might recommend the same changes for AAA-TV that she suggested in our example, but with the understanding that the fight could be long and hard to get to first place in the ratings. In fact, AAA-TV might have to be satisfied with second place in the market.

What it all boils down to is this: How much money is AAA-TV willing to invest to get to first place? A prudent general manager may decide to spend a little less on changes and be happy with second place. He may feel that the cost of trying to be number one is just too high and is not worth it. The general manager must have a realistic idea of how much money is available to invest in improving the newscast. The bottom line is that he'll have to do the best he can with what he has.

Obviously, when consultants work for stations in various markets, they encounter many different types of situations. The main things a consultant tries to do are discover what's wrong with a station and its news department, and then attempt to get the station owner or general manager to agree on a plan to fix the problem.

Many of the big-market stations and a number of the medium- and smaller-market stations hire consultants. It's now considered part of the expense of trying to stay on top. On the whole, consultants have helped develop television news into a much better product, one more in tune with what viewers want.

IV STARTING YOUR CAREER IN TV NEWS

10 Basic Abilities

There are some basic skills and attributes that every successful TV journalist possesses. Part of the process of deciding whether to pursue a career in TV news is to take a critical look at your specific strengths and weaknesses in order to determine your potential. On the basis of this assessment, you need to develop your abilities prudently in order to make the most of your own unique blend of skills and attributes. Some abilities are largely innate, whereas others can only be learned; however, almost all can be improved.

News directors constantly deal with college graduates who should have been told earlier that they were not cut out for on-camera TV news. But with their TV journalism degrees in hand, it's a bit too late to inform them their decision was a mistake. They will face great difficulties in developing on-camera careers. Some may make the transition to behind-the-scenes jobs such as producer or assignment editor; others will go into radio or print news. Career potential is a very touchy and perhaps arbitrary subject, but one that should be dealt with realistically. After all, one's potential will affect one's career to a great extent.

What About Voice and Looks?

If a person's voice isn't pleasant, and his or her appearance is not considered attractive by conventional standards, should that person pursue a career in TV news? This is a hard question to answer because news directors have different tastes; what does not appeal to one may be just what another news director is looking for. But there are minimum requirements. You don't have to have movie-star looks or a resonant voice to be a reporter or anchor. But there's no question that if a reporter has training, a decent voice, and an attractive appearance, these are certainly not going to hurt. We have to remember that TV is a visual medium, and appearance is a factor.

Of course, there are exceptions. You've probably seen TV reporters, or even anchors, who don't appear or sound particularly impressive but have other qualities that attract viewers. Maybe a certain anchor isn't good-looking but possesses an unusually engaging voice or style and delivers the news in a very concerned and credible way. Even though such people may be lacking in the looks or voice departments, they still have a certain appeal.

Make a realistic appraisal of your raw talent, including your appearance and the quality of your voice, and see if you feel there's a shortcoming. If you think you have a voice or pronunciation problem, you might consider taking an academic course or seeking other remedial instruction to improve your vocal quality or diction. Diction is very important because it's one of the main tools you'll be using as a reporter. It must be emphasized that radio and television news are not nearly as dependent on golden voices and glamorous faces as they were in the past. Nonetheless, your voice must be relatively clear and distinct so your story—the information you are communicating to the audience—won't be lost by being misunderstood.

How about looks? Can improving your appearance make your overall presentation better? Should you change anything about yourself? Again, you have to think about the competition—those other journalism grads looking for their first jobs. First focus on problems that can be changed relatively easily. Excess weight, for example, can be a drawback. On some people it is fine, but on others it may be unattractive. Your weight should not sap your stamina or hinder your ability to move quickly and easily—important requirements of a reporter. If weight seems to be an impediment to your presentation, you should work on the problem. Other factors, such as hairstyle, makeup, and dress, can have a significant impact on your appearance. Fortunately, cosmetic changes in these areas are easily achieved. If you find that your appearance undermines your presentation, there are many small changes you can make to produce a total positive gain. You may find some problems to be so severe that stronger steps are necessary. The extreme solution, of course, is plastic surgery, which some professionals have undergone. A great deal of thought and consultation should precede any major change.

You may be wondering how you'll appear and react when you're in front of a camera—what your "screen presence" will be. Everyone in TV news who works on camera has thought about it at one time or another—usually early in their careers. There's no doubt that some people seem to have a certain natural ability when appearing in front of others or on camera; they almost seem to thrive on it. But the fact is that most people in the business begin on shaky ground and simply improve with each on-air appearance. The smooth news anchors—Walter Cronkite, Dan Rather, Tom Brokaw, Peter Jennings, and many others—got that way through years of experience.

As they gain more experience, the best reporters and anchors become less concerned about how they look and sound. Their main purpose is to tell the story effectively so the viewers will understand it. And a funny thing happens along the way: the viewers feel they're watching a truly fine reporter or anchor. In other words, a genuine interest in informing the viewer will elevate a TV journalist above those reporters and anchors whose prime concerns are how they look and sound.

Reading and Writing

One of the biggest problems some students have today is poor reading speed and comprehension. If you're considered a slow reader, your time and money will be well spent if you enroll in a legitimate speed-reading course. After all, college requires a great deal of reading—not to mention the career you may be planning in journalism, which will call for continued reading throughout your life. The ability to read with some degree of speed will benefit you immensely, and most speed-reading methods enable you to retain much more of what you read.

Not only should you read well, but you should also be well read. Although a good college education will give you a broad background, you should continue to read and to learn about a wide range of subjects. As a reporter, the greater your breadth of knowledge, the more you will be able to ask informed questions and pinpoint the important issues in stories on various topics.

You will also work on your writing skills in school. Good journalists continually try to hone their writing abilities. Remember—even the best reporters can get better.

Other Abilities

The most important thing to keep in mind is that you will face competition every time you apply for a job. A station's news director wants to hire the best people he can find for the money the station can pay. The more valuable your assets, the better your chances of landing a good job.

Let's expand on the basic abilities needed for success in TV journalism. A common requirement, of course, is the ability to write and perform under pressure. One thing you can count on in TV news is deadline pressure! There are times when you'll have to run out on the set with only an idea of what you're going to say, or with your thoughts only partially scripted. The same thing can happen when you're doing a live report. You'll be fighting to get as much information as possible at the scene, and then all of a sudden there are only seconds left before you go on camera. Deadlines and deadline pressures are a way of life in the business—something you'll have to adjust to and accept.

Another important attribute is the ability to get along with just about anyone. Since you'll be talking with people from all walks of life in many types of situations and locations, this ability and a cool head will help you a great deal. Some reporting situations occur under stressful circumstances, whereas others occur under more relaxed conditions; each day brings something new.

As mentioned earlier, stamina is something every reporter must have. You never know when you leave the station what may happen—whether you'll be coming back later that day at a normal time, or whether you'll be heading out of town that night to cover another breaking news story. Long hours are a way of life in the news business.

Journalists need to have a sense of humor to weather the ups and downs of the business. This is especially true when things are a little slow (which happens every now and then). But remember, although things may be a bit dull today, tomorrow is another day and will probably be a lot different.

For the record, here's another undeniable fact that should go without saying: If you have a good, positive attitude and show a willingness to do your best with minimal supervision, you'll be among those preferred by news directors. A healthy and active curiosity is also a big plus. Such qualities can't help but carry over to both your audience and those with whom you work. These traits, as well as dependability, are truly essential.

And now for a word about teamwork: you know it's practiced by reporters and photographers, but it shouldn't stop there. Everyone has to cooperate if the newsroom is going to operate smoothly. One reporter may be through with her editing for the day, but another may need help with something. Maybe he just came in from covering a late story and has to locate some archive video. Whatever the scenario, teamwork is needed if the story is going to make it on the air for the newscast. Whoever is free should pitch in and do anything necessary. Remember, sometimes you will need assistance from your colleagues, so offer your help any time you see a need. The smaller the market, the more times you'll probably give help as well as receive it.

11 Educational Training

In the early years of TV news, network-level newspeople generally came from network radio news or newspapers, and most of them had journalism backgrounds. But on the local level, TV anchors usually rose from the ranks of local radio announcers, most of whom had little or no journalism background or training. (In many markets, local radio news in the fifties and sixties was primarily "rip and read"—the radio announcer or disc jockey ripped the news copy off the wire machine and read it on the air.) TV news is a lot different today. Now you must have some formal training in journalism, because almost everyone in the field does. Without it, you may have a tough time.

Testing the Waters

You've undoubtedly seen TV shows and movies that have depicted the activity in TV newsrooms and some of the work done by reporters, photographers, and anchors. The business looks exciting, but how can you be sure it's for you? Is there a way to get inside a TV newsroom to see what really goes on? Although you can get a close-up look at many professions today without too much difficulty, TV news is a little different.

TV newsrooms are somewhat closed to the general public. They're busy places, and the people who work there usually don't have time to stop and talk. There's also the matter of security; unwanted visitors have gotten into newsrooms and sometimes even onto the news set. One of the best-known cases occurred in Phoenix, where a man entered the newsroom, pulled a gun on anchorman Bill Close, and ordered him to read a statement. The incident didn't actually air (although the gunman thought it did), and the encounter ended peacefully. But to avoid such incidents, many newsrooms, and entire stations as well, are secured from the public.

Still, there are means of gaining some basic exposure to the business. The most obvious one is a formal internship program, such as those available through many universities (Chapter 12 is devoted to internships). Many of these programs, however, are not open to students until the latter part of a college degree program.

I urge you to gain early, practical exposure to TV journalism so that you can positively decide whether it is the right field for you before you invest several years in specialized study and effort. If you do decide on a TV news career, your early exposure can do nothing but bolster your experience. If an early internship program is not available, and if you persevere and use the methods outlined here, you may be admitted informally to a local TV newsroom to get a taste of the business.

If you live within driving distance of a city or town where TV stations are located, your first big obstacle has been overcome. Obviously, you need to be close enough to a station to commute. Call the news directors of the various stations. Tell them you're interested in TV news as a career and would like to come down and observe the operation. You might offer to help out on a regular basis in the newsroom as an enticement for the news director to accept your proposal. If she's agreeable, she most likely will want to meet with you before making any commitment. This need not be a regular internship—just an opportunity to observe newsroom activity for a few weeks or so. In a city with three TV stations, it would be surprising if you didn't get at least one acceptance out of three.

Keep in mind that even if nothing substantive comes of your meetings with news directors, you will still have had a learning experience. Your meetings can be what some career counselors call informational interviews. By being prepared and asking good questions, you can learn a great deal about the business in just one meeting. After several such meetings, you will have gained insight into how different news operations are run. These meetings also give you contacts in the business. Of course, the better you conduct yourself in a meeting with a news director, the better the chance that she will grant your request to observe the station on a more extended basis.

You will have more trouble contacting news directors in the larger markets. They're constantly besieged with applicants, and talking to all of them is virtually impossible. That's why many news directors have someone screen their calls. The standard answer over the phone is "Send us a tape and résumé and we'll get back to you." But you're not looking for a job, just exposure to the business. Make that very plain on the phone so you're not confused with a job seeker. If the news director isn't available, ask to speak with the assistant news director (if the station has one). If you still have no luck, then try the executive producer. But don't go too low on the staff; you want to talk to the highest authority possible. You may have to call back several times before you reach the right person.

Depending on the size of your community, the station may have neither an assistant news director nor an executive producer; there may be a combination news director/producer/anchor (indicating that this is a small market where you'll have a better chance at access). If that's the case, try to make an appointment by calling around 2:30 in the afternoon (this person will be very busy after 3 P.M.). You may be asked to come by the newsroom after the six o'clock newscast, when the rush is over and things are quieter. You'll be able to talk with fewer interruptions then. If you are accepted as an informal intern of sorts, make sure you show up on time, every time you're supposed to. This informal arrangement may help you get a regular internship later if you decide to pursue a career in journalism.

What if you don't live close to a TV station? Well, this will make your efforts to check out TV news a little more difficult. You may have to put it off a bit, most likely until summer. But if you live in a rural area not close to a large city and your college is also in a rural section, this does present a problem. Do you have a friend or relative who lives in a city or town with at least one TV station? Perhaps they will let you stay with them for part of the summer. If you can make such arrangements, your summer will be well spent. You won't learn a lot of specifics, but you'll be able to observe a great deal— probably enough to enable you to make your decision about a TV journalism career.

Before you make arrangements for your temporary move, be sure to call and verify that a news director will let you spend some time in the news department. Once plans are finalized on the phone, send a follow-up letter detailing what you agreed on, including when you'll be starting and how long you can work. Don't forget to include your phone number and address so you can be contacted if necessary. Your letter will serve as a good reminder.

It's important to remember that although most TV stations have news departments, some don't. Those that don't are generally independent stations not affiliated with a regular network like CBS, ABC, or NBC—so very early in your conversation, ask if they have a newsroom. In some big markets, independent stations do have news departments.

It's advisable to get a taste of the business no later than your sophomore year in college. That way, if you decide against a career in TV news, you will still have plenty of time to change majors. You need to be as sure as possible that TV journalism is for you. It would be a shame if you waited until your senior year to intern (or at least spend a little time in a newsroom) and then discovered you didn't like the business after all. What would you do? If you changed majors at that late date, you'd have to extend your stay at school.

To illustrate why early exposure to the business is important, let's take the actual case of a student from a major southern university. She was about to graduate and needed only six more semester hours for her degree in journalism. Her school wanted her to intern in a TV newsroom for two months (at 20 hours per week) to earn those six hours of credit. It was unfortunate that she had to wait until the end of her college career to get exposure to the business, but her school was located in an area with no TV station. In her case, summertime interning was also out of the question.

If only she'd had a chance to intern or work in a newsroom earlier, she would have learned enough about TV news to realize it was a career she shouldn't pursue. Of course, getting as much experience as possible by interning just before graduation (as she did) isn't a bad idea if you're sure TV news is for you. It may make looking for that first job a little easier because everything will still be fresh in your mind. But this particular student should have had some kind of practical exposure to the business before her senior year. Then she might have learned sooner that a career in TV news was not for her, and she would still have had time to change her major.

About a month into her senior-year internship in a TV newsroom, she decided against a career in TV. Although she showed promise as a reporter, she had looked closely at her potential and felt that she might not be able to progress to the type of position she wanted. Also, she had learned that she would probably have to move to a much smaller market for her first TV job. She said no one had told her about the difficulties and sacrifices involved when starting out.

Fortunately, this young woman's training was not really wasted. She landed a public relations position in which she was able to apply many of the skills she had learned in college and during her time in the newsroom. However, someone else might not have been so lucky. Do everything you can as early as you can to confirm your career choice.

If You're Still in High School

Throughout this book we've approached journalism through the eyes of a college student. But what if you're a junior or senior in high school with some interest in TV journalism but are unsure if you want to make it your career? As with college students, your decision will be easier if you can visit a TV newsroom a few times. If the town you live in has TV stations, this shouldn't be too difficult to arrange. But if you're in a rural area that's farther than driving distance from the closest TV station, it won't be practical to visit a newsroom at this time.

If your city or town has at least one TV station with a news department, it is probably best to have a guidance counselor or teacher from your school contact the news director to discuss your interest in journalism and your desire to observe the daily routine of a TV newsroom. More likely than not, the news director will agree to let you visit, perhaps during afternoons once or twice a week over a period of several weeks or more. Even though these few visits won't give you in-depth knowledge of the business, they should help to answer a number of your questions.

Not many high schools have formal internship arrangements, but some do have innovative programs for serious students who want to sample various career opportunities. Most news directors would be happy to cooperate with such a program. In some rare cases, a high-school internship might even lead to a part-time job.

What can you do while still in high school to prepare yourself for a possible career as a television journalist? There are a number of things:

1. *Work on your school newspapers* to gain practice in reporting, writing, and interviewing. It will give you a feel for what it is to be a journalist.

2. *Improve your skills in grammar and composition,* especially if you're weak in these areas. Good grammar and composition should become second nature to you; after all, they'll be essential tools in your career. If you wait until you're in your first job, or even until you become a journalism major in college, it may be too late.

3. *Try public speaking.* Most high schools have a public speaking group or club. Join it! This is an excellent way to build confidence and get a little voice training at the same time.

4. *Learn typing and word processing.* The benefits of these skills should be obvious. Certainly, they can be put to use no matter what you do in life. For reporters, they're essential.

5. *Watch TV newscasts.* This will keep you up to date on current events and the technology used by both local stations and the networks.

6. *Find a part-time TV or radio job* at a local station if your schedule permits. If you plan to get a part-time job anyway, why not one that will help you learn more about the business that may become your career?

You may not be able to implement all of these suggestions, but some should be possible. Part-time work at a local TV or radio station may be a little difficult to find, but you never know—so be sure to check it out! Part of being a reporter is having the tenacity to go back again and again to get the story (or whatever information you want). If one station says no to you on the phone, call the next one until you've called them all.

It would be a good idea to take some courses during your junior and senior years in high school that would help later in a news career. Political science, history, geography, and any writing courses would be especially useful.

Obviously, choosing a college is a key part of your high-school preparation for a journalism career. There are many books on this subject in your library, and high-school counselors will be able to assist you in selecting a college. Information on how to obtain financial aid for college is also plentiful at most libraries.

You may not be considering certain colleges and universities because you plan to attend the institution in your home town. A great many students do this for financial and other reasons. But before you make solid plans, check out your local college's bulletin to see if it has a journalism major. Don't assume that a small school can't offer the training you need. There are fine journalism programs at relatively small, and even low-cost, colleges and universities.

If at all possible, apply to schools that have full journalism programs rather than just a few courses. Substantial course offerings in the subject reflect a school's commitment to education in journalism. Also, be aware that some schools have a separate journalism department, whereas others make the journalism program part of the mass communication (or other) department. Although being part of a larger department may mean that the journalism program has access to greater resources, remember that the quality of the program itself is your most important concern.

Obviously, a wide range of courses will give you many options. You may be able to pursue either a major or minor in journalism, or even focus on a particular aspect of journalism—for example, producing TV news or reporting the news.

Many of the better journalism schools adhere to specific curriculum guidelines created by educational and professional organizations. Probably the most important of these organizations are the the Association for Education in Journalism and Mass Communication, or AEJMC (1621 College Street, University of South Carolina, Columbia, SC 29208-0251), and the Broadcast Education Association, or BEA (1771 N Street, N.W., Washington, DC 20036-2891). Both the AEJMC and BEA have listings of schools accredited under their guidelines, which might help you in selecting a school. Schools that have this accreditation have met very strenuous standards and thus generally have excellent programs. Of course, there may be some schools with good journalism programs that are not accredited.

As you consider schools and programs, be aware that there are many scholarships available for journalism students. The Radio-Television News Directors Association (RTNDA), for example, offers annual scholarships to prospective journalists. Your library and guidance center should have listings of these.

Finally, be sure that the schools in which you are interested can offer you a good, balanced education. A complete education for journalism includes more than just journalism courses. If you've been considering a number of schools, you should have already requested copies of their catalogs or bulletins. These will give you up-to-date information on courses, admission and graduation requirements, and a great deal more.

Do I Need a Degree in Journalism?

There are those who think a well-educated person with a minor in journalism but a major in a field such as liberal arts or political science makes the best reporter. Perhaps that is true in some cases. But you'll find that the majority of news directors who are hiring entry-level reporters prefer students with journalism majors. Remember, a news director is looking for the best-trained person available for the money the station can afford to pay. He or she may feel that an applicant with only a minor in journalism hasn't received enough training, no matter how well-rounded that applicant is. Most journalism degrees offer students plenty of time to get a broad-based education. Keep in mind that if your competition has a journalism major and you don't, he or she may have the advantage.

As a journalism major considering a minor in another area, you might want to choose a field that interests you as a possible alternate career or concentrate on courses that complement journalism. Public relations is an excellent field to minor in because many skills related to journalism and broadcasting can be put to good use in a public relations career. It's also a minor that is very compatible with a major in TV news. There are certainly many other interesting areas that would enhance your journalistic background. Courses in history, political science, English, and foreign languages, to name a few, would all complement the study of journalism. If you don't minor in any of these areas, at least be sure to include some coursework in a few of them.

What Can I Do While in College?

Up to this point, we've emphasized what you can do off campus in a local TV station to learn more about broadcast journalism. But there are plenty of things you can do on campus.

1. *Join your college newspaper and/or work in the college radio station* (if your school has one). Some schools even have TV editing equipment and makeshift studios. Working on the newspaper will expose you to interviewing and writing. A job with the radio station will help you learn to deal with various daily deadlines.
2. *Be well read.* Because you're going to be reporting about people and things around you, it will benefit you to be knowledgeable about local matters, as well as world and national news. Even though your first job may be a thousand miles away, local news tends to mirror itself in other cities. This is true whether the news concerns crime, government, taxes, school problems—you name it.
3. *Watch local and network TV newscasts.* You should become an avid viewer of your local stations' newscasts as well as network news programs. This will keep you up to date not only on current events but also on any new broadcast technology.
4. *Learn typing and word processing.* Everyone who works in a newsroom must know how to type. And with the advent of computers in newsrooms, computer or word-processing experience will be helpful.
5. *Polish your grammar and composition skills.* This should have been attended to in high school, but if there's still a problem, work on it. If you try to straighten out a weakness in this area late in college, you may find yourself getting bogged down.
6. *Get some experience in public speaking or debating.* This will be a big advantage in handling on-camera reporting after you graduate. Learning to speak in front of people will help to dampen any jitters you may encounter later as a reporter. Oh, you'll get the jitters anyway, but they won't be nearly as bad if you've had some practice in speaking before groups of people.

You may also consider becoming a student member of one of several professional journalism organizations. Such a membership would enable you to keep abreast of current developments in the industry and have access to other resources that could help you build your career.

The Radio-Television News Directors Association (RTNDA) is one organization that offers memberships to students. Student members receive a newsletter, job listings through the RTNDA placement service, and other publications. Membership is open to students who are at least college sophomores and costs approximately $40 per year. As noted earlier, the RTNDA is a strong supporter of proper training for journalism and offers several scholarships. Contact the RTNDA to get the necessary forms and information. (Address: 1717 K Street, N.W., Suite 615, Washington, DC 20006.)

The Association for Education in Journalism and Mass Communication (AEJMC) also offers student memberships, which cost about $30 per year. You'll receive several publications from them, including a newsletter every other month or so, and a quarterly report. (Address: 1621 College Street, University of South Carolina, Columbia, SC 29208-0251.)

Finally, the Broadcast Education Association (BEA) offers student memberships for $30 a year. Like the other organizations, they'll send you periodicals and other publications that will keep you in touch with the latest industry trends and issues. (Address: 1771 N Street, N.W., Washington, DC 20036-2891.)

I'm not suggesting that you join all these organizations, but you should be aware of them and perhaps pick one that you feel will offer you the most. A talk with a professor, news director, or advanced journalism student might help you make that choice.

12 Interning

The importance of either interning or working part-time in a newsroom can't be emphasized enough. Virtually all the professionals, and most journalism professors and department heads, agree that you need as much practical exposure to the business as possible *before* graduation.

In this chapter we will focus primarily on a formal college internship, not just a short-term visit to a newsroom. Note that an internship program should not be confused with a part-time job a college student might have at a local station, although the benefits to the student may sometimes be the same. In general, however, you'll probably learn more during an internship simply because it's designed specifically to teach you.

If interning will be your initial (and perhaps only) exposure to the business prior to graduation, try to do some of it during your sophomore year or the first semester of your junior year. This will give you time to change majors, or at least to make alternate plans for the future, should you decide against a career in journalism.

What Is an Intern?

An intern is a college student who works in a TV newsroom doing miscellaneous chores under the direction of some person in authority (generally the news director or producer). Interns generally don't do any writing or reporting, but they still get a great deal of exposure to TV news. News directors are usually delighted to have interns because both parties benefit. The interns help out in a meaningful way and get valuable on-the-job experience in return.

In rare cases, interns receive pay for their work, but this is the exception rather than the rule. Interns are generally not paid. They work a specified number of hours a week for a certain number of weeks. For this they normally receive 3 to 6 semester hours of college credit, depending on what their schools allow. Because of the great distances interns may have to commute in larger markets, some large-market stations give their interns a small stipend for bus, subway, or train transportation.

Some TV stations have very specific requirements for interns. They insist that anyone interning must receive college credit. This means that once you've earned the maximum number of credits your college will allow for interning, the station may not be able to use you anymore. Why? Because federal law mandates that a student not receiving college credit in an internship program must be paid at least minimum wage.

While you're interning, you'll have the chance to learn many things that should eliminate problems after you graduate and begin working full-time in the news business. The more experience you have, the more prepared you'll be by graduation day. Most news directors take note of how much interning or other work an applicant has done in a news department, because they know it makes you a better-trained and more valuable candidate.

Getting an Internship

Be sure to carefully research any internship that is available through your school. In this way you may find out valuable information about the newsroom, its staff size, and the person to contact at the station regarding the internship. You might even discover evaluations of the internship by students who have already worked at the station. This will give you a good idea of what to expect at a particular station and whether past interns have had positive experiences there.

Call the contact person (and also the news director, if it's not the same person) to verify the information you have and obtain information you lack. Ask specific questions about the station's internship program: What are interns allowed to do? Can they get actual hands-on experience? The responses you get will help you decide where you'd prefer to intern.

If you're planning to intern in a market larger than the 50th in size, be sure to ask if there is a union and, if so, whether this will prevent you from doing certain types of work (chances are you won't find a unionized station till you get above the 40th market). A number of unionized news departments do not permit interns to do any writing, reporting, editing, or anything else that actually goes on the air. Unions are concerned that if no restrictions are put on interns, the station could simply bring in more of them to handle the workload and let some of the regular staff go.

However, if you're planning to intern in a medium or smaller market (most likely any market smaller than the 50th in size), there probably won't be a union. In this case, you might be allowed to do almost anything (to a point) based on your abilities. Some smaller-market news departments have permitted their best interns to report and edit packages that actually aired!

In order to intern, a student must obviously be located within a reasonable distance of a city or town with one or more TV stations. If your college is close to a metropolitan center, you'll probably be interning while school is in session. But if your college is not near a TV station, you may have to arrange to do an internship during your summer break.

Schools far from TV stations often have formal summer internship programs. You may also be able to earn credit for an internship you arrange yourself if you get advance approval from the proper authorities at your college. Your journalism department or advisor may be able to help you develop such an internship. Start early and call the news directors at the stations near your home or near any other place where you can spend the summer with friends or relatives.

Some schools won't let students take journalism courses till the sophomore year, which may mean they won't recognize interning done earlier. Don't fail to verify with your college that you'll receive credit if you plan to do any early interning.

Some colleges and universities have very strict requirements for interning. In these cases, you can't just visit the head of the journalism department and expect to be given an internship; they're usually awarded only to the best students. This leaves a number of others out in the cold. Where are they to go? Are they expected to forgo an internship altogether? If you are unable to get an internship from your college, then you must forge ahead and try to find one on your own (although it will be unofficial and you won't receive credit).

There may be other internship-type programs available that don't provide college credit but do offer meaningful work experience (as well as modest pay). Schools often have listings of such positions. Or you may be able to obtain a part-time job in a newsroom to gain the exposure you want. Even colleges with no formal internship program are usually happy to help students find noncredit work experience. Regardless of the pay issue, the point is to get as much exposure to the business as possible so you'll be better prepared for the future.

Learning from Your Internship

As mentioned earlier, what you'll be able to do during your internship will depend on the size market you're in, whether there's a union involved, and the station's own policy toward interns.

Let's assume you're in a medium- or smaller-market station where no union restrictions apply. Before you arrive in the newsroom, check with the news director for guidelines on exactly what he'll allow you to do in your first few weeks. As he sees how you progress, he may gradually let you to do more things. Chances are, at this station you'll eventually be permitted to do some writing and editing if you show enough capability. If it's a small market, you may even get to go out and cover some of the not-too-complicated stories. It will all depend on how much training you've had at school and what abilities you demonstrate to the news director. Obviously, a sophomore intern would not be expected to go out and do a package on a story, but a senior should be able to.

It's very important for you to listen to what's going on in the newsroom—what the reporters and photographers are saying. Much of their conversation will concern the events they've covered that day. You'll hear about what happened on the various stories, as well as the difficulties involved in covering them. Some day you'll be a reporter, doing the same things and running into the same difficulties. Having heard how experienced reporters and photographers dealt with various situations will make you better prepared to handle similar ones.

When reporters or photographers are very busy and news time is fast approaching, it's best not to bother them with questions. Try to ask earlier in the afternoon when things are a little calmer and people are not so rushed. Most newspeople are happy to answer an intern's questions, especially if they sense you're very interested in the business and are eager to learn.

At some point you will probably be allowed to go out with a reporter and photographer as they cover a story. Watch what they do and listen to what they say. When you arrive at the event, carefully note the questions the reporter asks. You should also take a notepad along and cover the story yourself. When you get back to the station, try to write the story (not a package, of course, but the general story). Then compare what you've written to what the reporter writes. This way you'll begin to learn how to pare down what may be complicated issues into simple and easy-to-understand reports.

The more you can do as an intern, the better prepared you'll be to deal with your first job. Try to take advantage of every opportunity you're given so you can show the news director how interested you are in learning and how well you can handle the job.

As mentioned previously, if you're interning in a union station, there may be a number of restrictions on what you can do, both inside the newsroom and while out with a news crew. It's very important to find out the guidelines regarding what you will be permitted to do in a union newsroom. It will eliminate problems later.

Despite the restrictions, you can still learn a lot in a union newsroom. As with any news department, you can listen to and talk with the staff about their problems and how they handle things. You will probably be allowed to go out with a news crew and observe how stories are covered (remember to carry your pad along and take notes). You can watch the editing process back at the station and compare your story with what the reporter wrote. You can also rewrite wire copy for practice and compare your own style with that of stories already written from past scripts. If you have a good rapport with a particular reporter, have her check your stories and make comments.

If you're interning in a unionized newsroom, it's probably in a fairly large market, and you may not be able to get feedback from the news director. However, in many large-market newsrooms there is a staff member with the title of intern coordinator, or at least a person in charge of the internship program. Go to this person for answers to questions about what you're doing or to find out who to see to have your writing critiqued.

Regardless of the type of newsroom you're in or what you're allowed to do, interning will be a very important learning experience for you. You're observing the real thing—exactly what you'll be doing when you graduate. You can absorb a great deal from simply watching, asking questions, and remembering. You'll probably look back on your days as an intern as some of the most productive in your undergraduate experience.

13 Your First News Job

It will be an exciting day when you get your degree and begin the search for your first TV news position. Your job market is the entire United States! As you know, the average market has only three TV stations (maybe less) with a limited number of reporting and photography positions. As a result, you should be prepared to move anywhere in the country for your first job. If you live near a large market, a move is almost a certainty, because you won't have the experience the news directors in that large market are looking for. This is something you'll have to tell your family to expect.

Contacting stations six months before graduation may be a waste of energy. Stations that hire beginning reporters receive countless résumés and tapes all the time. Yours will just end up in another pile in the news director's office. A news director generally won't start looking for new help until one of his staff members gives him a letter of resignation. About two months before you're ready to go out on interviews is the earliest you should start contacting news directors; make it plain in your letter that you will be available very shortly.

At a seminar in San Francisco, a news director told how he routinely threw away any correspondence from applicants who either spelled his name wrong or addressed it to a former news director. This remark might be considered somewhat arrogant, but it is a little careless to misspell the name of the person you're trying to contact. If you've gotten the news director's name over the phone, double-check the spelling with the person to whom you're speaking. If you've obtained the name from a published source—an ad in *Broadcasting* magazine, for example—it might be a good idea to call the station to verify the spelling.

Broadcasting Yearbook is a helpful publication that will save you a lot of time and expense. In addition to containing a wealth of information about radio and TV stations, market sizes, cable TV, Federal Communications Commission (FCC) rules, and much more, the *Yearbook* also includes listings of each television station and its news director, address, and phone number. Many applicants get news directors' names out of the *Yearbook* and send out mass mailings. Unfortunately, because TV news is a volatile business as far as job stability is concerned, sending out letters this way is bound to result in a number of them being addressed to news directors who have left the station. It's impossible for any annual publication to maintain a truly up-to-date list. Keep this in mind when you're planning your résumé mailing list.

Cover Letters

As you're no doubt aware, your cover letter should be short—no more than one page—and spelling and grammar must be checked very carefully. The number of letters sent out with misspellings is shocking. For a college graduate to mail a letter with such errors suggests carelessness or a lack of knowledge and makes a bad impression on most news directors. Some might figure that a person who is careless enough to send out a letter with misspellings or grammatical errors would probably be a careless reporter.

In your letter, mention any intern work you have completed and note what you've done in a newsroom (even though this should also be included in your résumé). Outline any accomplishments you feel will help to sell yourself and be professional in your approach. Don't try to grab attention with some bizarre statement in the opening line of your letter. A news director may immediately dismiss a letter that begins with something like, "You have in your hands a letter written by the best young reporter you can hire." Believe it or not, letters like that do cross news directors' desks. Originality is one thing, but that type of cover letter will probably backfire.

It's preferable to "shoot where the ducks are," so to speak, and send out smaller mailings only to those stations that you know have openings. Mass mailings can be expensive and the results negligible. Later, if you've exhausted all leads and have some postage and résumés left, you can consider sending out general mailings.

Summary of Cover Letter Tips

- Double-check the spelling of the news director's name.
- Double-check the spelling and grammar in your letter.
- Keep your letter short—no more than one page.
- Avoid trying to be different in an effort to impress.
- Don't promise more than you're capable of delivering.

Résumés

Résumés, like cover letters, should be as short as possible—preferably one page. Many news directors prefer résumés that begin with your most recent experience and go backwards in time. Of course, if you're a new graduate you probably won't be able to list a broadcasting job, but you may have some intern experience. Include other jobs you have held and briefly describe your duties for each one. Also be sure to list all of your extracurricular activities in college. This will give the news director a little more insight into the type of person you are.

If you've written for a college newspaper or have any print experience, be sure to mention it. Most news directors feel that a print background is not a handicap but, in many cases, a big plus. Although newspaper stories are usually longer than TV stories, newspaper writing is excellent training for a career in TV journalism. That's because writing is everything with a newspaper. Unlike TV, there's no video or sound to help tell the story; the writing has to carry it all.

It isn't necessary to have your résumé printed on fancy colored bond paper. A news director is primarily concerned with what your résumé tells her about your training and experience. However, a résumé on colored paper will tend to stand out a little more in a pile of others. Above all, make sure your résumé is neat and easy to read.

Sending a résumé without a cover letter is not advisable. It's far too cold, like mail addressed to "resident." A letter to the news director, along with a résumé, will at least establish some kind of personal contact. You may be calling the news director later to touch base with her. Chances are she'll remember you a lot better if a letter was included with your résumé.

Consider sending a recent photo if you feel you're attractive or think a picture can reveal something that's unique about you. That's really the only reason for the picture—another way to sell yourself.

Finally, list the names of references—people for whom you've worked—at least for your last job. If you don't have much (or any) work experience, then list the names of professors who know you. But as far as a news director is concerned, your best reference is a former employer.

Summary of Résumé Tips

- Keep it brief.
- List your most recent job experience first.
- Include extracurricular activities.

- Make sure the résumé is neat and easy to read.
- Include a cover letter with the résumé.
- Consider including a photo of yourself.
- List references.

Résumé Tapes

When you begin your job search you'll be sending out a cover letter and a résumé, but ideally you'll also be able to include the single most important thing an aspiring TV journalist can supply a news director—a videotape résumé of your stories.

You'll make a much stronger impression with a tape in addition to your written résumé. It will help make you stand out and will show the news director how you look, how you sound, and how much poise you have on camera. Obviously, if you're applying right out of college, she'll know you haven't worked as a reporter yet. But the tape will give her a better idea of your potential and may enable her to advise you about your future in the business, even if she doesn't hire you.

Now you're probably saying, How can I, as a student, put together a résumé tape when I've never worked as a reporter? Well, there are ways to get at least something of yourself on tape.

First, let's assume you're a journalism student with a year or so of college left and you've arranged to do an internship at a TV station somewhere, even if it's just for the summer. The news director there may make it possible for you to do some on-camera anchoring for your tape (in many cases, this will be easier for you to arrange than going out on stories). If you're fortunate enough to be allowed to observe a reporter covering a story, you can take notes and write your own version, using the raw videotape shot on the story. Many news directors will allow you to put together a tape in this way. They know how important it is for you and are usually willing to help, as long as it doesn't interfere with the day's newsroom activities.

If you have a few stories to put on tape, position your best first, the next best second, and so on. Varied types of stories (hard news, feature, and the like) will show your versatility. But don't bother with more than three; that will be plenty for a news director to look at. If you have only one or two stories and they're all the same type, go ahead and put them all on your tape—one or two stories are better than none. Follow them with some anchoring if you can.

A news director who likes what he sees in the first few minutes or so will keep looking. He'll be able to spot the raw talent he's looking for very rapidly if you have it. It may be the sound of your voice, your delivery, the way you present yourself on camera—but he'll know quickly. That's why it's important to put your best work first.

If you're a graduate who didn't have an opportunity to intern, putting together a tape will obviously be a little harder to manage. Here's a suggestion: if you live near a TV station, call the news director and tell her you're a journalism student who hasn't been able to intern. Ask if you can come by and see her newsroom, or perhaps observe it for a day or so during the afternoon hours, when the news is being put together. If you live in a large market, arranging such a visit may be more difficult. But you'll be surprised at how many news directors are willing to let a student drop by.

Toward the end of your visit, ask the news director if it would be possible for you to sit on the set and tape a few minutes of yourself anchoring several stories. It will be more difficult for her to turn you down face-to-face than over the phone. If she grants your request, make sure you're well rehearsed, because she may want to do the taping right away.

The station's cameras will probably have TelePrompTers. As you look at the TV camera, you will see your script on the TelePrompTer, which is located in front of the camera lens. This will seem a little awkward at first, but you'll probably get a chance to do a dry run or two before the taping. The more you practice reading your script at home, the smoother it will go in the studio.

Be sure to take a VHS cassette in case the news director says you'll need to supply your own tape. However, she may end up giving you a ¾-inch cassette, which is what you want anyway. That's the size tape used in most newsrooms and is of higher quality than VHS. You can offer to pay for it, but she'll most likely decline accepting payment.

At this point you might be pushing it if you ask for any *dubs* (copies) of your tape. You might call the newsroom one night after this visit and talk with a reporter or photographer. Explain your situation and ask if there are any old tapes around that can be used to make dubs of your tape (most newsrooms have plenty of tapes sent in from public relations firms and the like). Most likely, after you offer to pay the person to dub your tape, he or she will agree to do it and may not charge you anything.

It should be noted that the response you will get to your request for a newsroom visit may vary greatly from station to station. Some news directors may turn you down flat; others may let you come by but may not be willing to let you anchor stories for your tape; others will help you as much as possible. You won't know until you ask. The worst that can happen is for the news director to say no.

If your college has some videotape equipment, you may be able to complete an anchoring segment on campus. Depending on the type of recording equipment at your school, you'll wind up with either a VHS cassette or a ¾-inch tape (the latter, as mentioned earlier, is what you need for the best quality). Be sure enough lights are set up to give you the best possible picture. If you can't get dubs of your tape made at your college, you may be able to have them done at a TV station or cable company, or by a production company or advertising firm with the necessary type of equipment.

Be sure to put your name, address, and phone number on the tape itself. Your cover letter and résumé already contain this information, but they could become separated from your tape. Also, don't expect to get your tape back immediately. It may be returned in a week, several weeks, months—or maybe never. News directors are deluged with tapes and sometimes misplace them.

Summary of Résumé Tape Tips

- Put your best story first, second best second, and so on.
- Use no more than three stories.
- Include an anchoring segment at the end (if available).
- Total length should be no more than 10 to 12 minutes.
- Put your name, address, and phone number on the tape.

Before You Begin Your Hunt

Now let's get down to the process of job hunting. Here are some things to consider before you embark on your search:

1. Hunting for a job in TV news is harder now than in the past, simply because today there are fewer TV news jobs and more applicants looking for openings.
2. Realize that you may have to move to a much smaller market than you expected, and it could be on the other side of the country. This is a significant factor that every journalism student needs to be aware of before making a career decision. Moving around the country is a certainty in TV news, and anyone disinclined to relocate should think twice about a career in TV journalism.
3. If you limit your job hunt to a specific section of the country, you will severely limit the number of job openings for which you may be considered.
4. You may have to be a one-man band in your first job, so become familiar with electronic news-gathering (ENG) cameras and recorders while you're still in school.
5. At first you may have to work for surprisingly low wages and at odd hours. But look at it this way: it's your first job, and you're still learning. Your first job is more or less an extension of college.

If you can come to grips with these facts, you're ready to begin your search. You must realize that if you interned in, say, a 50th-market station, it is unlikely that you'll get a job there. Even if you're especially talented, you still don't have enough experience for the news director to hire you. Remember, there are countless reporters in the smaller markets who have both the experience and the ability for which the news director is looking. After you spend a year or so in general-assignment reporting in a smaller market, you'll be ready to move up. It can't be stressed enough how much 40 to 50 hours a week of covering all kinds of stories will sharpen your talents.

Getting Down to Business

There are many possible job-hunting techniques. Entire books have been written on the subject, and many of them are quite helpful. Use whatever resources your school has; many have career centers that provide guidance and job listings. You will probably need to go much further than this, however. The following suggestions are geared specifically to job hunting in the field of TV journalism.

Check Broadcasting Magazine

You've probably seen more than one copy of *Broadcasting*, the industry weekly magazine. Although there are others, it's the one that for years has had the most job openings in its classified section. It should be checked every week. Since many of the jobs listed are in medium-to-smaller markets, it's ideal for your purposes. Also, *Broadcasting* has a section in the back of each issue called "Fates & Fortunes." It lists people who are moving from one job to another and notes the jobs they've left, the new positions they've taken, and the stations involved. This can be a good source of job leads.

Let's say you're looking for an entry-level reporting position. You scan the listings and find that someone is leaving a job in a small-market station for a medium-market reporting job (for example, say they're going from market number 150 to market number 90). You then call the station this person has left and inquire whether they have any openings. You may find that the job is wide open. But it's important to note here that "Fates & Fortunes" listings are supplied by either the person changing jobs or someone in the promotion department at his or her new station. For this reason, you may often find these listings to be a little outdated; the job may have been filled weeks before you read about it. Don't worry, though   sometimes you'll run across a job that's still available. As mentioned earlier, you can get all the phone numbers you need from *Broadcasting Yearbook*.

Use Broadcasting Yearbook

The latest issue of *Broadcasting Yearbook* is at your library. You may even want to buy it; although the *Yearbook* is fairly expensive, it contains a wealth of information about the stations and markets in which you're interested. Let's take an example:

Assume you've called a station and found that it needs an entry-level reporter. You turn to one section in the *Yearbook* to look up the market size for that station. In another section, you'll see a small map showing the counties served by the stations in the market. Next to this is a listing of all the stations in the market, their channel numbers, and their network affiliations, if applicable.

What can you learn from all this? First of all, the market size gives you an idea of the town size. Obviously, any market close to number 200 is a pretty small area. If the market is large—say, number 47—you'll know your chances of being hired are slim, because a market that big will want applicants with more experience than a recent graduate.

What else can you learn? The channel number can tell you something about the station. Let's assume our market has three network affiliates, two of which are on channels in the VHF range (channels 2 through 13) and one of which is in the UHF range (channel 14 and above). If the opening is with the UHF station, you'll know it is probably not the leading station in the market. Why? To a large degree it involves TV reception. Ask almost anyone without cable TV service and they'll tell you how difficult it is to get a UHF signal with any quality. For those who have cable, every station's signal is equal, so to speak. But many people still do not have cable, so their TV antenna is the only way they can receive signals. Many TV antennas, although said to be designed for both VHF and UHF, in fact give a much better VHF picture. Just check around to see how the UHF stations are doing in relation to their VHF counterparts, and you'll find the UHFs are almost always behind the others in their TV newscast ratings. This really shows up when a market has only one UHF station and the other two are VHFs; however, if a market is composed of all UHF stations, you won't find this disparity.

You may have your best shot at a job at a UHF station, assuming it's a network affiliate. That's because stations in third place, regardless of their channel number, usually have smaller staffs, and smaller salaries to match. The news director has to hire less-experienced applicants because he just can't afford people with more experience. This creates more entry-level job opportunities—and possibly an opening for you. Remember—if you're looking into a UHF station, be sure to find out whether it's a network affiliate. As mentioned earlier, a number of UHF stations are independents with no network affiliation, and these usually don't have news departments.

Subscribe to Medialine

Another source of job openings is Medialine, a telephone job bank to which you can subscribe. You simply call in at any time to hear about the latest job openings. Medialine is more immediate than any classified section. The number is 1-800-237-8073 (1-408-296-7353 in California).

Call The National Association of Broadcasters' Job Line

The National Association of Broadcasters (NAB) has a job line in Washington. It functions much like Medialine, but the service is free. It operates on weekdays from 6 P.M. throughout the night until the next morning at 8:30, and all day Saturday and Sunday. However, not all openings are listed each night—one night is sales, another engineering, and so on. News openings are announced on the NAB job line from Friday night at 6 P.M. until Monday morning at 8:30. From Monday night to Tuesday morning, openings for on-air talent are announced. The job line number is 1-202-429-5498.

You may call the main number of the NAB during the day to check which jobs are listed on which nights. The main number is 1-202-429-5497.

Call News Directors

Although it can be a little frustrating, another method of getting the latest in job openings is to call the news directors at any stations in which you may be interested. Most news directors are very busy, but you may be able to get through to some. Some news directors have a policy of not talking with applicants unless they've sent a tape and résumé, whereas others may be glad to talk to you. As noted before, news directors in the larger markets are the least accessible and may be almost impossible to contact. But when you can't talk to the news director, ask for the assignment editor or the producer. Either one will probably be able to tell you whether there are any openings.

Send Résumés

Still another method of job hunting is to send résumés to all the stations in all the markets in which you're interested (that may be more than 150!). But the problem here is that news directors get so many résumés, yours may be lost in the shuffle. Also, this method may be the least productive for all your effort. You're "shotgunning" a bunch of stations without knowing whether there are any openings, and you may be wasting a lot of time and postage. If you do use this method, make sure you send a cover letter, and possibly a photo, to make your presentation more special than many of the others.

Meet News Directors Face-to-Face

One final method of finding openings takes time and money, but it may be productive. You can drive from city to city and try to meet the news directors at various stations, let them see you in the flesh, and leave a tape (if you have one) and your résumé. As costly as this may seem, many graduates invest their time and money doing it. The simple reason is that it puts you in the news director's office; a face-to-face encounter makes a much stronger impression than a résumé. Countless news directors have hired people because they came in at the right time *and* had the necessary qualifications.

Summary of Job Search Tips

- Check *Broadcasting* magazine weekly (it's mailed out every Monday). Don't forget the "Fates & Fortunes" section for leads.
- Call Medialine regularly (you must pay for this service).
- Call the NAB job line in Washington (free).
- Call TV stations, using numbers found in the *Broadcasting Yearbook.*
- Send résumés to a number of stations (get the names and addresses from the *Broadcasting Yearbook*).
- Take a tour of a selected section of the country, stopping to see news directors along the way.

You may not be able to follow all of these tips—especially traveling from city to city—but try as many as you can; your chances of getting a job will be improved. You may have some other ideas of your own.

Don't forget friends in the business who may know of an opening—it pays to keep in touch. Incidentally, some heads of journalism departments have contacts in the business and may be aware of openings as well. You'll have to use as many approaches as possible to find your first job. And you must persevere: there are fewer jobs out there now, so you have to work hard to find one.

The Interview

Let's say you've found a job opening. Now what? If you've been granted an interview, carry along an extra copy of your résumé in case it should be needed.

Also take a copy of whatever videotape you have of yourself. Even though you've already sent one, the news director may have misplaced it, so the copy may come in handy during the interview.

What's the news director going to be looking for in you as a candidate for an entry-level reporting position? Her prime interest will be whether you can write well. This skill is probably the single most important thing news directors hope to find. Any interning you've done will be noted because this relates to actual newsroom experience. A call from the person interviewing you to the news director at the station where you interned will give her an idea of what kind of worker you are and whether you perform well under deadline pressure (newsrooms need people who don't "lose it" when things get a little rough). She'll also observe your overall energy level and sense whether you seem enthusiastic about joining her news department. Obviously, your personal appearance should be at its best, and a friendly, cooperative attitude will go a long way in your favor.

She knows you don't have true 40-hour-week experience—after all, you're looking for your first job. But she is interested in your raw qualities, some of which will be apparent on your videotape (if you have one), and others that she'll be able to ascertain during the interview and from your résumé. Your references will help her find out more about you too. They can shed light on your overall work habits and how you get along with coworkers.

At this point you're excited, and you probably want the job, regardless of the circumstances—especially if you've been job-hunting for a while and this is your first real possibility. But what should you be taking note of while the station is looking you over?

You might notice how well-kept the outside of the station is as you arrive for the interview. Almost all stations make sure things look good out front; a shoddy exterior appearance may indicate problems inside. Don't worry too much about the appearance of the newsroom—it's likely to have a very "lived-in" look. What you want is a sense of how well organized it is. If it's a small news department, the news director will probably also be the assignment editor. This may mean he'll have to pause occasionally while talking with you to check something on the police scanner. You'll undoubtedly get a tour of at least the newsroom and most likely the rest of the building too. See what state the editing booths are in—the condition of the equipment and how worn it looks. The master control area is another place management likes to keep in first-class shape. If it looks dilapidated, that's a negative sign.

With all this said, however, your decision really depends on how badly you want the job, if one is offered. Remember, this is your first job; you won't be there the rest of your life. You need the chance to begin working as a full-time TV journalist as soon as possible. During your initial year you'll grow tremendously in the business; after that you'll be ready to move up and on to a better job. In a very real sense, your first job is a type of postgraduate work.

Some Thoughts on Your Future

Once you've landed your first job in TV news, you'll soon begin to look forward to the next one, hopefully in a larger market. This is natural; we all want to move ahead both professionally and financially. You may also tend to think that as you move into the bigger markets, you will run into nothing but the best-trained and most talented people. That's generally true, but not always. Now don't misunderstand—there are many talented people in the bigger markets. News directors aren't in the habit of hiring poor-to-medium talent in a market where news involves big money in both revenue and salaries; they want to hire the best people they can get. But still, some very average people do slip through. Television news is a little like Hollywood in that the best actors don't always get the starring roles. In TV news, the best anchors and reporters are not always the ones holding down jobs in the big markets.

Many reporters reach a point at which they know they're as good as (or better than) some of those they see working in larger markets. If they still haven't advanced as fast or as far as they had envisioned, they may become frustrated (as can happen in any business or industry). Of course, as we all know, life isn't always as fair to us as we would like. There's an element of luck in TV news as in any other business. Often, being in the right place at the right time can make all the difference in someone's career. The point is this: be prepared for some ups and downs.

No matter how hard you try not to, you'll make plenty of mistakes in your first year—it happens to everyone in the business. However, the more interning experience you've had, the fewer mistakes you're likely to make on fundamentals. Remember, you're still learning and will continue to learn, especially in the early years of your TV news career.

In live television anything can happen when you least expect it, so be prepared. Remember Murphy's Law: "If something can go wrong, it will go wrong." So when you make a mistake, don't fret over it too long. Just remember what you did wrong—and be consoled in the knowledge that many others before you have made the same mistake, or much worse.

V THE FUTURE

14 What Lies Ahead?

We've spent a lot of time talking about TV news as a career. But with ratings, consultants, and everything else, you may be wondering how long such a career can be expected to last. Well, that question is hard to answer in just a few simple sentences. To a large degree, your ability to make TV journalism a lifetime career will depend on two basic things: first, the type of position you'll hold in the newsroom in later years, and second, the success of your station in the market and whether it has demonstrated a long-term commitment to news.

The point is, if you're at a good station, your chances of making a career out of anchoring (or any other newsroom job) are good too. But if you're at a station that's struggling in second or third place, your job may be less stable. Obviously, anchors and news directors are in the most danger of being fired if the ratings are too low. Reporters, photographers, and producers generally have safer positions (assuming they're doing a good job) and are less likely to get the axe.

For most people who work in the newsroom, there are only two ambitions: to anchor or to be a news director. All the other positions are used as stepping stones to reach one of those goals. If you want to work on the air, you'll begin as a reporter and, with any luck, move on to anchoring one day. If you want an off-the-air career, you will probably begin as a reporter but later move on to be an assistant producer (or perhaps a producer in a medium market). From there, you'll work your way up through other off-air jobs in the newsroom on your way to becoming a news director.

Anchors

When ratings fail, an anchor may not be at fault but may still be in danger of getting fired. An anchor's career depends to some degree on ability, but almost as much on the ability (and the audience's acceptance) of the co-anchor and the weather and sports anchors. As discussed in Chapter 8, a station's ratings are often affected by how much money it spends on promotion. In addition, as noted in Chapter 5, other factors include how well-staffed the newsroom is (as compared with its competition), how skillful the news director is in keeping the newsroom running smoothly, how much energy and persistence the assignment editor puts into coordinating all the daily newsroom activities and keeping the reporters turning out good stories, and numerous other things that are not the anchor's responsibility.

An anchor is literally at the mercy of all these factors. No matter how good one is at anchoring or how hard one works, the ratings could slip because of problems in any or all of the areas just mentioned, as well as changes in the station's degree of commitment to its news department. Remember, too, that anchoring involves a bit of show business, and no matter how diligent an anchor is, the audience may simply prefer someone else.

Some anchors are quite successful simply because their stations have a long history of "doing things right"—spending money when necessary and always maintaining a top-flight news product. An anchor hired by this type of station is probably talented anyway but will also have the added benefit of her station's momentum—a momentum built up over many years of proper management. The anchor may think she is responsible for the continued high ratings, whereas in reality, the station's loyal viewers may have merely accepted her as a member of their favorite news team and not as the main attraction.

Many anchors work at a half dozen stations or so before they reach the point where they feel at ease about settling down. They may not be totally satisfied with their situation, but they realize they've probably reached the apex in their career and have a job worth holding onto. At this point, moving to a bigger market may not be possible. If so, they must accept this and ask themselves whether they'll be content to stay put for the long term. If the answer is no, they may consider getting out of the business, but that's not what generally happens. If the market they're working in is large enough to pay them well, and if the station is a good one, they'll probably stay.

It's hard to predict at what age an anchor will have to step down. Some very successful stations have long-time older anchors who are still on the air. But remember, if there's any ratings problem, an anchor (regardless of age) had better plan for a possible job change, because his days may be numbered. You can see why it's difficult to count on anchoring until the end of your career. There are just too many variables.

News Directors

The job of news director is usually one of the two most sought-after positions in a TV newsroom, anchor being the other. Yet news directors have one of the highest termination rates of all news personnel. It's been said that the average life of a news director is two and a half years at any one station (of course, there are many exceptions). When new management comes into a station that's been doing poorly, the standard practice is to replace the news director and possibly one or more of the anchors (although that may take place later, after a new news director has been hired). The other staff members (assistant news director, assignment editor, producer, etc.) are not considered to be as responsible for any problems and are generally allowed to stay, assuming they do their jobs well.

Are There Safe Jobs?

People with certain jobs in the newsroom are not in as much danger of being fired as the news director or assignment editor, for example. Almost invariably, these people don't make any management-level decisions in the newsroom.

The "safer" jobs are essentially off-air: photographers, reporters (even though they are seen on the air), producers, assistant producers, and the like. Generally, the off-air positions with more responsibility, such as assignment editor, executive producer, and assistant news director, are a little bit closer to the firing line—but they're still well behind the news director and the anchors in terms of susceptibility to termination. Let's take a closer look at these positions and see what kind of future they might offer you.

Reporters

Good reporters are generally in a less precarious position because they're not considered to be a turn-on or a turn-off for viewers. A reporter who does a decent job in a professional manner is relatively safe. But although it's a more secure job, the money may not be enough to support a family unless you're at a big-market station. That's usually why older reporters are rarely found anywhere except in the bigger markets.

However, large-market jobs are very competitive, with many people going after few job openings. This leaves lots of reporters of all ages out of luck. Therefore, except in the larger markets, a reporter who has reached his late thirties will generally have done one of three things: become an anchor, left reporting for an off-the-air job, or abandoned the business altogether.

With only a slim chance of moving into the big markets, an experienced reporter (if good enough on camera) may have the option of anchoring in a smaller market. Regardless of age, a reporter who is unable to locate a job as a reporter or anchor in a larger market, or can't become an anchor in a medium-sized or smaller market, may be forced to leave TV news for economic reasons. This is why reporting is rarely a long-term career; it's simply part of the process that leads (for some) to anchoring. The only problem is that there are relatively few anchor positions as compared with the large number of reporters, so the competition is very intense.

Photographers

If you want to be a photographer, you probably should think of that as a temporary career too. After being in the business for a while, most photographers want to move up and out of shooting. Carrying that heavy equipment around can be tiring, and most eventually want to trade it in. However, a photographer without a journalism-related background or some college training may not be able to move to another position in the newsroom.

Other Jobs

While other off-the-air jobs (such as producer or assignment editor) pay better, they still may not offer the money necessary to support a family unless you're in a relatively large market. So, as with other TV positions, you need to gain experience in the smaller markets and continue to move ahead until you reach a market in which the station and the money are satisfactory. At this point you may consider yourself to have a safe job if the ratings are good and you're good at what you do.

Job Stability

Whereas age is not a big factor in off-the-air positions, competence is. You need to remember there are many young people entering TV news today, and employers know they can always find someone to do the job cheaper.

Let's break down the various positions into the categories of least stable, more stable, and most stable. This is pretty much how it stacks up at most stations:

Least Stable
1. News anchors
2. Weather anchors
3. Sports anchors
4. News directors

More Stable
5. Reporters
6. Assistant news directors
7. Assignment editors
8. Executive producers

Most Stable
9. Producers
10. Assistant producers
11. Photographers
12. Production assistants
13. Newsroom secretaries
14. All others

Most anchors choose to continue anchoring, even though the job frequently lacks stability. The pay is always better, as is their professional status in the business. News directors also seem to roll with the punches and don't worry too much about the axe falling. Along with the anchors, they are the best paid, and they too have status.

It's a pity that you can't just settle down in a local TV newsroom in the city of your choice and make your career there, but that's seldom possible. Since there are few jobs and many applicants, you have to take the position that seems best for you, no matter where it is—and it may be 2000 miles from your home!

In summary, your chances of making a long-term career out of TV news will be greater if you choose either reporting or off-the-air work. These positions are less susceptible to firing and should be relatively stable for people who do a good job.

15 Career Changes and Alternatives

Most people who enter the field of TV news never expect to leave the business, but it does happen. Young reporters usually think they'll anchor in a large market one day, or maybe even at the network level. Producers hope they'll wind up being news directors in a large market. But the fact is that TV news, like most other industries, just doesn't have enough upper-level jobs to go around.

Because of this, a number of people in the business decide the time has come to move on to new challenges, while others lower their career sights and adapt to their situations. Some are able to change to another newsroom job that offers more satisfaction. For example, an assignment editor may be tired of the stress of the job and move into producing. An anchor who's dissatisfied with his career advancement may decide to become a news director. But for others, TV news loses some of its luster, or at least some of its initial attraction. These people probably need a change. Let's take a look at the various other fields that are particularly open to people who've worked in TV news.

Public Relations

This is an area especially well-suited for newspeople from TV as well as from radio and newspapers.

Some public relations (PR) firms, and PR departments in certain companies, don't deal with the media to a great extent. They may exist primarily to facilitate communication within a company (by producing company newsletters, for example). However, most PR firms and PR departments deal extensively with print and broadcast media. As a PR person, you'll probably write press releases, set up news conferences, and the like.

As a former newsperson, you'll have the special know-how required to get the most mileage from the media. After all, you've been there: you know what to put in a press release, and how to come up with a news angle that will make an assignment editor or news director more receptive. Anyone who's spent time on the assignment desk at a TV station and dealt with incoming press releases knows that many of them are wasted effort by the PR firms, advertising agencies, or companies involved; most go into the trash. Obviously, many of the people preparing them don't know what information TV news needs or how to come up with some news that would justify a story. A great many former TV and radio people work in PR because their news experience is of great value in that field.

TV Sales

Many people in TV stations feel that sales is "where the money is." It's probably true, because salespeople generally make more money than most other employees of a station, except perhaps the station manager or sales manager. This is not usually true at first, of course, but those who stay in sales for a while are generally quite successful financially.

Countless people have changed jobs within the same station by giving up TV news for TV sales. Others have left one station to work in the sales department of another. One thing you need to keep in mind about sales: you'll probably be working on a commission basis, with perhaps a small draw against sales. As in many sales positions, you're likely to go through some lean times, especially at first.

Starting out in sales can be rough because new salespeople are usually given accounts that haven't been "worked" for a while—accounts with companies that may have advertised on the station in the past but decided to stop at some point. That decision may have been made either because the company felt the advertising was ineffective or because it had run out of money to spend on TV advertising. Or perhaps the former salesperson didn't always keep a close watch on the commercials the station ran for a particular client. The ads may have aired at the wrong time or had technical problems. The client may have noticed such mistakes and become disgruntled because the salesperson failed to straighten them out.

Many people will tell you that sales is an exciting field. For some this may be true, but for others the constant possibility of rejection may be too hard to take, and they'll leave sales, perhaps to return to the TV newsroom.

Management in TV or Radio

Some news directors have actually been made general managers of their stations. In the 1970s this was rare, but the number of former news directors in the "GM" ranks is growing. Some newspeople have switched to a department-head job, such as production manager, within the same station.

In many cases, your exposure to the various facets of the business (although you've primarily been in the newsroom) could give you the edge over someone else trying to come in from outside the station. Besides, many companies like to promote from within. But be realistic—if you've been with a TV station for a year and a half and decide you don't like TV news, you shouldn't expect to be considered for a management-level position in another department. Department heads generally come only from the ranks of those who have demonstrated their competence in the business for at least several years.

Press Secretary

This is another position for which TV news experience is an excellent background. As a matter of fact, most successful press secretaries have worked in TV or radio news or on a newspaper. Politicians know the power and importance of the media, and they want someone with the knowledge and experience to get the most from the press. Mayors of cities of all sizes have a staffer who deals with the press. Many county executives also employ people to handle those duties. Of course, governors, as well as US senators and members of the House, all have press secretaries. Someone who's worked as a reporter or assignment editor will have dealt with people in these offices and made some contacts. Through such contacts, many a reporter has moved on to a position as press secretary in a mayor's office, a governor's office, or even higher.

The problem with these positions is that they may be short-lived. After all, you're a press secretary for someone only as long as they're in office. If they lose an election or retire, you'll be out of a job unless they've helped you locate another position. When press secretaries lose their jobs, they usually find other newly elected officials who need an experienced hand. These officials generally prefer someone who knows Washington or the state capital and already has some contacts (this assumes that you're of the same political affiliation, of course).

You may say, that's fine, but I'm working on the local level; I have no experience outside my own area. Well, a newly elected member of Congress may decide to take a friendly local newspaper or TV reporter to Washington as his or her press secretary, despite the experience others might offer. This has happened before. Members of Congress often want their press secretaries to know something about the district back home, and someone who's spent most of their time in the nation's capital won't have that qualification. Governors have also taken press people from their home towns with them to the state capital.

A press secretary's life can be an exciting one. The hours are often long, and there may be weekend work and travel—but if you've spent any time in a newsroom, this will probably not be a problem.

Wire Services and Newspapers

This is another area in which you can apply your skills as a reporter and writer. After all, you have dealt with the wire services on a daily basis and are familiar with how they operate. This is one position you may be able to step into easily.

TV Consulting

As mentioned in Chapter 9, a number of former TV newspeople have gone to work for consulting firms. Ex–news directors, as well as other experienced people in the business, find this is an excellent career alternative. It's not for everyone, but if you possess demonstrated ability and knowledge, can impart it to others, and like to travel, this field may be ideal for you.

Other TV Jobs

The career options we've discussed in this chapter are those that are compatible with training and experience in TV news, but you may not be interested in any of them. If that's the case, you may want to investigate a field of broadcasting in which you have no direct experience, such as programming or operations.

Think carefully before you make a decision to move into a field completely unrelated to TV. Let's say you've spent five years as a TV reporter and are in your late twenties. If you choose to pursue a public relations career, much of your background will be transferable, and you'll be able to make a smooth transition (with some minor adjustments). But if you decide to enter a field that is totally new to you, such as the insurance business, you'll literally be starting out all over again. Granted, your ability to deal with people may help, but the work will be completely new; it will almost be as if you've just gotten out of college. Can you afford to backtrack like this?

Leaving the TV newsroom is a big decision, and one that should be very carefully weighed. Once you've left, it may not be easy to get back into the business, because there are countless job-seekers just waiting for any position that might open up. However, a surprising percentage of people who leave TV news do return. They find that nothing else offers them the same rewards. Even though they may not be strongly attracted by the pay, they're drawn back into the business; being away from it makes them realize how much they miss it.

Glossary

Anchor   The person who delivers the news, weather, or sports during a TV news program. In small markets this individual also may be the news director and producer.

Assignment editor   The person responsible for sending out news crews to cover the day's events, monitoring the police scanners for breaking stories, and, in general, coordinating daily newsroom activities.

Assistant news director   Second in command to the *news director*. This position is nonexistent in most small markets because of budget constraints.

Assistant producer   The person, not usually found in smaller markets, who works under a producer and handles many daily newsroom chores related to getting the newscast on the air.

Beat calls   Telephone calls made each day by reporters or the assignment editor to see if any news stories are developing on the police, city hall, court, and other beats.

Beat system   The system in which reporters are assigned specific areas (or beats) to cover, such as courts, police, city hall, and schools.

Backgrounder   A story concerning the history (recent or distant past) of a person, group, object, place, etc.

Betacam   A camera, videotape recorder, and battery supply combined into one lightweight unit, developed by Sony.

Bite   A script that begins with the anchor relating part of the story. Videotape then appears on the TV screen with a knowledgeable person commenting about the news event. Also known as *sound bite*.

Break   A commercial break in a news or entertainment program.

Cable TV   Television news and entertainment programming sent into homes by a special cable installation.

Cassette   In television news, a plastic cartridge holding videotape for news

139

and sports stories. Cassettes used by photographers covering news events are usually 20 minutes long, but some special tapes are 30 minutes long. Other cassettes in use at TV stations vary in length from 5 to 60 minutes.

Character generator   The electronic device that places *supers* on a TV screen.

Closed circuit   A program or information, not for broadcast, which is sent by a network to its affiliated stations. It may be an advisory about programming changes or an episode of a new show scheduled to air in the future, among many other things.

Computerized newsroom   A newsroom that uses computers instead of typewriters to write stories and to accomplish other tasks. The wire services, such as AP and UPI, are sent electronically to the computers rather than being printed out on paper as in the past.

Consultants   Specialists hired by station management to evaluate a station's overall image and the performance of its news department in comparison with competition in the same market. The consultants recommend ways to improve the station's operation and its news ratings.

Cut-in   Generally, one of several short local newscasts that air in the early morning network news programs.

Demographics   The breakdown of viewers by age and gender for any particular program. This information is ascertained during the ratings process.

Director   Not to be confused with the *news director* who heads a newsroom, the director is responsible for giving the newscast the most professional look possible. In some stations the directors also perform all the electronic switching needed to put the anchors on the air, run videotape, and other things essential to the newscast.

Documentary   Usually, one long report—perhaps a half hour or an hour—on a single topic. Similar to a *series*.

Editing   The process of selecting and electronically putting together the best scenes on videotape for a story.

ENG   Electronic news gathering. All of the videotape gear today's news and sports photographers use in covering stories.

Executive producer   The person who supervises newscast producers in a news department and ultimately is responsible for how each newscast looks on the air. This position is not found in smaller markets.

Features   Stories that usually are done on lighter or "softer" subjects. They can, however, be serious and thought-provoking.

Feed   Usually, the transmission of stories to a station by a network or other news service through a special telephone line or by satellite.

Folo   A story that updates viewers on a previously aired story.

General manager   The person who runs the entire station and is responsible to the owners for its success or failure.

Hard news   News of a violent or dramatic nature, such as a fatal car accident or a murder trial.

Incue   Generally, the first few words of a sound bite used in a news story.

Independent   A TV station that is not affiliated with one of the major networks such as ABC, CBS, or NBC. These stations have to program their entire day, whereas a network affiliate runs programming supplied by the network during most of the day and evening.

Intern   Most often a college student working in a newsroom to learn what the television business is really like. The intern usually receives college credit plus the advantage of practical on-the-job training.

Investigative reporter   One who works on special stories involving more extensive research into a subject or individual than normally would be found on a typical news story.

Live shot   A live report from the scene of a news story that is in progress or has already occurred.

Live van   The vehicle holding the remote live reporting equipment such as the transmitter and antenna. The van transmits the signal in a straight line or "line-of-sight" path back to the studio, free from such obstacles as buildings or tall trees.

Market   In television terms, a market is any of the approximately 210 geographic areas in the continental United States that are served by TV stations.

Microwave   Usually refers to the transmitter used in live vans or satellite trucks to send the live report (signal) back to the studio (or to a satellite) where it can be recorded or broadcast live.

News director   The individual in charge of a news department who is responsible for its overall news effort. In small markets this person also may be the news anchor and producer.

One-man band   A reporter in a smaller market who doubles as a photographer. Also may be a photographer doubling as a reporter.

Outcue The last few words on a *sound bite, VO-bite,* or *package.* It's necessary that the newscast director have this information in order to know when to cut away from the videotape and go back to the anchor on the set.

Package A story done by a reporter on videotape. The anchor begins by reading an introduction (intro) to the report, which includes the reporter's name. The entire story is narrated by the reporter, complete with interviews and other pertinent videotape of the story.

Photographer In TV news, one who photographs the day's news events with a videotape camera.

Producer The person responsible for ensuring that the many elements of a newscast are assembled properly so it will have a polished and professional look.

Production assistant Sometimes confused with the assistant producer, the production assistant usually handles the more basic chores in the newsroom, working under a producer or assistant producer.

Promotion As it pertains to television news, the effort of a TV station to attract more viewers by making them aware of its news anchors and news programs.

Rating or Ratings points Unlike *share,* the actual number of people watching a television program. For this reason, the rating is extremely important to advertisers.

Ratings The process of measuring the number of people watching the various television programs to determine the size of each show's audience. This information also is broken down into categories by age and gender.

Reader The simplest type of script in TV news—a story read by the news anchor, with no videotape seen on the screen at any time. Sometimes referred to as a liner.

Re-cut Refers to re-editing a story for a later newscast.

Reporter The person who covers the day's events with a photographer and makes sure the stories are written and edited properly for the evening newscast. In many smaller markets, a reporter who must double as a photographer is known as a *one-man band.*

Résumé tape A videotape cassette showing the best work of an applicant for a news job. The résumé tape is perhaps more valuable than a written résumé since it is a better indication of a person's abilities.

Rundown Generally, the list of stories to be aired on any given day and the order in which they'll run during the newscast.

Satellite Circling the globe, satellites have many "channels" or "paths" that receive signals from earth and then retransmit them back to the ground.

Satellite truck   A vehicle outfitted with the electronics necessary to send signals to a satellite. Satellite trucks are used instead of live vans when great distances must be covered or when there is no line-of-sight path to send the signal directly to the studio.

Script   The common news scripts—*readers, sound bites, VO-bites,* and *packages*—are defined in detail in Chapter 3.

Series   A group of reports, generally running a week or less, on a particular subject.

Share   The percentage of viewers actually watching a television show in relation to competing programs. Does not indicate the total number of people watching, just the program's standing relative to its competition.

Sidebar   A story done as a spin-off of another, such as a *backgrounder.*

Sound bite   This script begins with the anchor reading on camera as in a *reader.* At some point the anchor stops and videotape appears on the screen with someone commenting about the story. Also known as *bite.*

Spot news   This is a news event that occurs suddenly and without warning, such as a fire, auto accident, or shooting.

Stand-up   Every time a reporter is seen on camera during a story, it is considered a stand-up. It may be located at the beginning, in the middle (usually called a *bridge*), or at the end of the report.

Supers   A name seen at the bottom of a TV screen that identifies either the person speaking on camera or the location of a scene shown in a news story.

Tags or "Tagging-out"   Usually, a news anchor's final words at the end of a story. Sometimes, the reporter's outcue on a package—the last thing he or she says.

TelePrompTer   A device in front of the studio camera lens that allows anchors to see the news copy and relate it more effectively to the audience.

Translators   These electronic devices receive a station's signal, strengthen it, and retransmit it to a rural area that otherwise might have no television reception. Since the signal is retransmitted on a different channel, it won't intefere with the main station's signal, even if it's weak.

UHF   Ultra high frequency. All channels numbered 14 to 83.

VCR   Generally, home videocassette recorders, which can be used to tape television programs, most often from cable.

VHF   Very high frequency. Channels 2 through 13.

Video   Vidcotapc of any news or sports story.

Video archivist   Found in larger stations, the person responsible for saving and keeping track of all videotape stories used in every newscast.

Videotape Widely used to record news events and entertainment programs on TV, videotape has virtually replaced film, except for some commercials and other special programming such as documentaries.

VO Voice-over. Similar to a *reader* script. Shortly after the anchor begins the story, the viewer sees videotape of what the anchor is talking about.

VO-bite A combination of *reader*, *VO*, and *sound bite*. The story begins as a reader, but then videotape appears on the screen as in a VO. A short time later (5 to 30 seconds) a sound bite appears.

For Further Reading

Biagi, Shirley. *Interviews That Work: A Practical Guide for Journalists*. Belmont, CA: Wadsworth, 1986.

Bliss, Edward J. and Patterson, John M. *Writing News for Broadcast*, 2nd ed. New York: Columbia University Press, 1978.

Chancellor, John and Mears, Walter R. *The News Business*. New York: Harper & Row, 1983.

Cohler, David Keith. *Broadcast Journalism: A Guide for the Presentation of Radio and Television News*. Englewood Cliffs, NJ: Prentice Hall, 1985.

Cohen, Akiba A. *The Television News Interview*. Newbury Park, CA: Sage Publications, 1987.

Fang, Irving. *Television News/Radio News*, 4th ed. St. Paul, MN: Rada Press, 1985.

Garvey, Daniel E. and Rivers, William L. *Newswriting for the Electronic Media*. Belmont, CA: Wadsworth Publishing, 1982.

Graber, Doris A. *Processing the News: How People Tame the Information Tide*, 2nd ed. New York: Longman, 1988.

Hilliard, Robert L. *Writing for Television and Radio*, 4th ed. Belmont, CA: Wadsworth, 1984.

Hood, James R. and Kalbfield, Brad. (eds). *The Associated Press Handbook*. New York: Associated Press, 1982.

Hough, George A. *News Writing*, 4th ed. Boston: Houghton Mifflin, 1988.

Hyde, Stuart W. *Television and Radio Announcing*, 5th ed. Boston: Houghton Mifflin, 1987.

Keirstead, Phillip O. (ed). *The Complete Guide to Newsroom Computers*, 2nd ed. Overland Park, KS: Globecom Publishing, 1984.

Keith, Michael C. *Broadcast Voice Performance*. Boston: Focal Press, 1989.

Kessler, Lauren and McDonald, Duncan. *When Words Collide: A Journalist's Guide to Grammar and Style*. Belmont, CA: Wadsworth, 1987.

Lewis, Carolyn Diana. *Reporting for Television*. New York: Columbia University Press, 1984.

Mencher, Melvin. *News Reporting and Writing*, 4th ed. Dubuque, IA: William C. Brown, 1987.

Metzler, Ken. *Newsgathering*, 2nd ed. Englewood Cliffs, NJ: Prentice Hall, 1986.

Orlik, Peter B. *Broadcast Copywriting*, 3rd ed. Boston: Allyn and Bacon, 1986.

Stephens, Mitchell. *Broadcast News*, 2nd ed. New York: Holt, Rinehart and Winston, 1986.

United Press International. *The UPI Broadcast Stylebook: A Handbook for Writing and Preparing Broadcast News*. New York: United Press International, 1979.

White, Ted and Meppen, Adrian J. *Broadcast News Writing, Reporting and Production*. New York: Macmillan, 1984.

Yorke, Ivor. *The Technique of TV News*, 2nd ed. Boston: Focal Press, 1987.

Index